D0907025

LEGACY

PRAISE FOR *LEGACY*

"In this insightful and much-needed book, Richard Orlando, trusted advisor to many of the world's wealthiest families, shares the essential strategies he uses to help his clients make value-driven decisions about managing their wealth and establishing a meaningful multigenerational legacy."
  —**Chip Conley**, *New York Times* bestselling author of *Emotional Equations*

"Richard Orlando's financial management advice shows we can live a connected, service-oriented life in touch with our values while building an enduring family legacy of success. Orlando provides critical guidance for navigating major life decisions to make sure they strengthen relationships rather than driving families apart."
  —**Keith Ferrazzi**, *New York Times* bestselling author of *Who's Got Your Back* and *Never Eat Alone*

"I've long been an admirer of Dr. Orlando's groundbreaking work helping families integrate their spiritual and financial ideals. His book is an excellent resource for those who still feel there is something important lacking in the wealth management experience."
  —**Hannah Shaw Grove**, author of *The Family Office*

"Richard Orlando's new book, *Legacy* brings into our consciousness the fundamental role of spiritual capital in a family's flourishing and in the happiness of its individual members. Richard teaches us that when a family's human, intellectual, social, and financial capitals are joined with its spiritual capital it stands a strong chance of avoiding the universal cultural proverb 'short sleeves to shirt sleeves in three generations' and the suffering it defines. My reading of Richard's book affirms my strong belief in his conclusion and its message offers great value to families everywhere and their advisors."

—**James E. Hughes, Jr.**, author of *Family Wealth* and *Family*, and coauthor of *The Cycle of the Gift*

"Richard's book brings a new and challenging perspective to the estate planning profession. *Legacy* is filled with stories, principles, and a framework for those of us who want to expand our value to our clients. In particular, the chapters on wealth transfer and preparing the next generation make a compelling case to factor the next generation into the planning process. I would recommend this book to every advisor and family who is ready to look beyond conventional wisdom as they plan for their legacy."

—**David A. Stein**, partner and head of U.S. Wealth Planning, Withers Bergman, LLP

"Given the uncertainty and volatility of the financial markets, Richard Orlando's book is a beacon of wisdom, savvy, and experience for legacy and investment managers. It is the ultimate wealth preservation and growth book for all to savor or aspire to. I recommend it highly."

—**Ernest D. Chu**, author of *Soul Currency* former Wall Street Journal staff writer, former member of the New York Stock Exchange

"I have had the privilege over my professional career of advising many families on their wealth transfer decisions. It is always very complex, as no two family situations are the same and there are seen and unseen dynamics at play. Dr. Orlando approaches this topic with wisdom and principles based on considerable experience. This book should be a very valuable resource both for professionals and anyone with wealth transfer opportunities and issues. I recommend this book with enthusiasm."
> —**Ron Blue,** founder of Kingdom Advisors and Ronald Blue & Company

"A MUST-read. It will forever change the way you think about your family and estate."
> —**Paul A. Pagnato,** managing director and partner, Pagnato-Karp Group, a Barron's 2013 top 100 financial advisor

"Richard Orlando provides practical wisdom and excellent insight into the complex set of subjects surrounding legacy planning. He expertly argues the what, how, and why questions, pointing out that optimizing these decisions is about intellectual, social, human, and spiritual capital, not just financial capital. Recommended reading for anyone serious about the subject of legacy."
> —**Bob Doll,** chief equity strategist and senior portfolio manager, Nuveen Asset Management

"Richard's passion for helping people navigate the ever increasingly complex world of financial choices is laudable. His approach demystifies and simplifies, giving investors the peace of mind they deserve."
> —**Elliot Weissbluth,** CEO of HighTower

"Dr. Richard Orlando's book, *Legacy*, provides the necessary guidance to help families optimize their family wealth decisions and prepare their family for the wealth. In particular, his focus on next-generation preparation does an excellent job of pointing out what wealthy families need to provide to their children. Following Dr. Richard Orlando's 'Ten Principles and Practices for Parents to Raise Their Children's Life IQs' is a great place for parents to begin this process."

 —**Rowland M. Smith III, C.P.A., CSEP, M.S.T.,** tax partner
  at ParenteBeard LLC

"As CEO of an international company, I have read many books on leadership, wealth, and success. Of these, Dr. Orlando's book is in a class by itself. *Legacy* provides principles and insights that can assist business owners and entrepreneurs in their pursuit to prepare themselves and their children for the opportunities and responsibilities that come with success. This book is a must-read for anyone interested in creating a positive legacy through their company and family."

 —**John Rakolta, Jr.,** CEO of Walbridge

"After playing basketball in the NBA for the past twelve years and now planning for the next stage of my life, I couldn't have read a better book. It is filled with practical wisdom that's guiding me and my family from success to significance. I wish this book would have been available earlier in my career. I strongly recommend it to professionals who want to make the best possible decisions regarding their wealth, success, and family."

 —**Michael Redd,** former NBA player (2000–2012) and
  member of the USA National Men's Basketball Team
  (gold medal winner, 2008 Summer Olympic Games)

LEGACY

The Hidden Keys to Optimizing
Your Family Wealth Decisions

Richard J. Orlando, Ph.D.

Legacy Capitals Press
New Hope, Pennsylvania

ISBN 978-0-9894810-0-7 (hardcover)
ISBN 978-0-9894810-1-4 (paperback)
ISBN 978-0-9894810-2-1 (ebook)

To my family

Twenty percent of the profits of this book will go to charity.

CONTENTS

Introduction *1*

PART ONE   THE ROAD LESS TRAVELED

Chapter 1   Navigating Your Legacy 15

Chapter 2   Preparing for Your Legacy Journey...........37

**PART TWO   LANDMARKS ON YOUR FAMILY
             WEALTH JOURNEY**

Chapter 3   The Pursuit of Happiness...................... 53

Chapter 4   Transferring Your Wealth......................71

Chapter 5   Next-Generation Preparation 97

Chapter 6   Giving and Sharing 127

Chapter 7   Taking Care of the Business of the Family ... 145

Final Thoughts..*167*

Acknowledgments..*169*

Notes *173*

Resources *181*

About the Author..*183*

Index *185*

INTRODUCTION

Live your legacy.

F amily life is a journey with predictable milestones: Every fork in the road, speed bump, and change of direction requires a decision to be taken. Whether it is a decision related to the recent global financial crisis or a liquidity event, a marriage or divorce, a death, the birth of a baby, a career change, or some other issue, *all* individuals and families will face important successes, conflicts, and transitions that impact our wealth. As our wealth rises, it magnifies any relationship issues that exist among our family members, blurs the lines between love and money, and makes decision making more complex and sophisticated.

How you plan for your legacy and answer the five most important family wealth decisions will directly impact you and your family for generations to come. My purpose in this book is to help you and your family lead flourishing lives in the context of wealth. This book will help you know how to answer these five questions, as well as secure the reason for your answers.

Too many people are misinformed. Legacy planning is *not really* about making an end-of-life plan or focusing on which fi-

Legacy is about how we choose to live each moment of our lives.

nancial assets we will leave to our heirs and charities. Legacy is about how we choose to live each moment of our lives. In this sense, planning is not about *leaving* a legacy, but about *living* our legacy. It is about reaching our human potential and intentionally making a positive imprint on the world each day of our lives.

Most of us do not have books written about us when we die celebrating our individual accomplishments, vision, and philosophy, like Steve Jobs. Still, Jobs is a great example of someone who has a powerful and far-reaching legacy. The impact of his legacy began decades before his death and created ripples around the world, and not only in the technology sector. As an inventor, an entrepreneur, a filmmaker, and a philanthropist he touched so many people's lives that after his death Harvard Business School's *Working Knowledge Newsletter* printed a special section entitled "The Legacy of Steve Jobs." In one of the articles for this special section, Regina Herzlinger, a faculty member at Harvard Business School, is quoted as saying:

> *The life of Steve Jobs is like a biblical saga. A mighty prophet emerges, visionary and charismatic, but he is imperfect. He deserts early allies (Steve Wozniak) and has other troubled relationships. He is widely spurned because he is so harsh and demanding. He is in turn betrayed by his closest ally (John Sculley), but ultimately the clarity of his vision and charisma triumph, and he transforms the world. The transformation in communications he creates gives ordinary people the voice to topple mighty business-*

es and governments. Would you expect any less from a mighty prophet?[1]

Whether you find Jobs' example inspiring or intimidating, because he set the bar so high, the point is that he didn't know his ultimate legacy when he began his career and experienced his setbacks. He lived his life step by step, decision by decision, just as the rest of us do, guided by his talents and interests. In the process of living, he made his mark.

Like Jobs, all of us are creating legacies for ourselves, whether or not these are intentionally planned for, or will be captured retrospectively someday in a book, magazine article, or movie. In *Legacy: The Hidden Keys to Optimizing Your Family Wealth Decisions*, I'm going to encourage you to think about your family wealth decisions in the context of your legacy. In these pages, I encourage you to answer what I believe are the five most important family wealth questions in terms of their meaning, value, and purpose.

1. How do I ensure a happy and fulfilled life for myself and my family?
2. How do I transfer my wealth to my children and others I care about?
3. How do I prepare the next generation in my family for the opportunities and responsibilities of wealth?
4. How do I best give and share my resources with others?
5. How do I ensure that my family business (whatever it may be) flourishes?

THE ORIGINS OF THIS BOOK

Over the past quarter of a century, I've worked alongside, and for, financially successful individuals and families from around the globe, paying keen attention to the attributes that led to lives that flourished in the context of success. I have wondered why some seem content in their success, why others seem to be motivated more by fear than love, and how they answer questions such as those posed above. Among other types of professionals, my clients are entrepreneurs, corporate executives, and professional athletes, some managing first-generation wealth and others managing second-, third-, fourth-, or fifth-generation wealth.

I have functioned as an educator, a business consultant, a life coach, and a trusted advisor to some of the wealthiest families in the world. I have sat with such families in their living rooms and boardrooms, reviewing their balance sheets, estate plans, and life plans, and having conversations with them about what matters most to them. They've shared with me their visions, philosophies, heritages, values, hopes, and dreams, and their deepest fears and struggles. In addition, I've trained, coached, and collaborated with other trusted advisors who serve affluent individuals and families. In this book, I intend to share with you my discoveries from helping my clients, as individuals and families, make their decisions.

Legacy planning is spiritual in nature because it ultimately starts with intentions and wishes that transcend the tangible world and are imprinted on the lives of others. Having said this, tangible assets that allow for outcomes such as the creation of a vaccine to cure a disease, the purchase of a home for loved ones to dwell in, or providing water and food for the impoverished are manifestations of an intended legacy to positively impact the lives of others. Utilizing global positioning technology as a metaphor for navigating the decisions that lead to your legacy, I will show you how and why your *spiritual capital* is the most powerful GPS navigation tool to optimize the way you and your family make your most important family wealth decisions.

I'm going to use the concept of spiritual capital throughout this book, so let's take a moment to understand the concept. Spiritual capital is a metaphor for the spiritual dimensions of our lives, our spiritual resources, as being a form of capital. Although the concept of a divine spirit or God has been around since the beginning of time, the concept of intangible spiritual resources as being a form of capital in the same way that financial resources like cash and hard assets are capital is relatively novel in the context of family wealth.

Spiritual capital is one of five types of interdependent capitals, or resources, each of us possesses. Wealth, in the form of money, property, and other tangible assets—in other words, our *financial capital*—is another. Ironically, the greater our financial capital, the more complicated it is for our family to answer the five most important family wealth decisions; however, the more we invest in our spiritual capital, the easier it is. Money is like a magnifying glass: With money, every issue—whether emotional, relational, social, or legal—is increased in scale, complexity, and sophistication. Your spiritual capital balances out the complicating impacts of your wealth.

In this book, I present a framework for understanding all the capitals an individual and a family possesses, including *intellectual capital, social capital,* and *human capital,* as well as the financial capital and spiritual capital we've already mentioned. I also make the case that, of the five types of capital we possess, the most powerful resource is our spiritual capital, although it is the one most of us typically invest in least often. By incorporating our spirituality—our values, purpose, and faith—into our decision-making systems, we can experience lasting happiness, successfully transfer wealth across generations, harmoniously work in business with our family members, and leave behind a positive social legacy.

Our decisions will not be optimized unless we have a proper

understanding of legacy planning, factor all our capitals into our family wealth decisions, and allow our spiritual capital to guide the process. These are the hidden keys of legacy.

WISDOM

I recently heard a speaker talk about wisdom. The speaker said what we all know: Wisdom is applied, or practical, knowledge. But he went on to say something much more insightful when talking about the laws in our country. Paraphrasing him, he said that we couldn't have enough laws to cover every potential action or decision taken by people. We sometimes need wisdom to act and decide in those gray spaces between and outside the laws. There is a profound similarity in how many people make their five most important family wealth decisions solely by adhering to the laws, or rules, that are available and not by intentionally using their value-driven spiritual capital to make them wisely.

Conventional estate planning is done rationally and intellec-tually—and understandably so. An estate attorney, for example, brings a legal and tax lens to the issue of wealth transfer, primari-ly with the intent of, let's say, helping create an estate plan to min-imize taxes paid to the government upon death and to protect assets from debtors and creditors. But unless the conversation and lens is broader than that—and incorporates core values and personal wishes, such as how to prepare the next generation for the assets versus only preparing the assets for the next genera-tion, and so forth—the estate plan could be missing crucial ele-ments that are important and meaningful to the family's legacy.

I can remember walking down the driveway of a beautiful estate toward my car after spending the afternoon with an ex-tremely successful entrepreneur named Thomas, talking about everything from his financial assets to his family relationships. Thomas was hospitable and open during our discussion of what was most important to him. I'll never forget the last words he said as I was getting into my car to head back to my office, "Like everyone else, I fear I can lose *all this* tomorrow." Thomas was referring to his estate and the significant wealth he'd created. While having a restless, almost paranoid fear of "losing it all tomorrow" is not uncommon among wealth creators, especially first-generation and second-generation wealth creators, Thomas was mistaken about one thing: Not everyone else feels the way he did.

By contrast, I can remember walking into my first family meeting with the Bairds. There were twenty family members in the room, representing three generations, joyfully greeting one another. Grandfather Baird, the patriarch, opened the meeting by reading inspirational words to his offspring. After the gathering wrapped up on day two, I remember heading back to the airport thinking, "I was asked to come and serve this family, but they ultimately served me." Watching them engage with one another, make decisions together, observing how every family member had a valued place at the discussion table, hearing them openly describe their perspectives on life and work, and sensing the family's genuine love of one another and contentment across the generations was both impressive and encouraging. Their open and loving interactions and the positive energy in the room gave me energy and a fresh reminder that a family of wealth can be successful *as a family* even in the context of significant wealth. Family is one of my highest values, so I appreciated knowing that by taking a values approach the influence of wealth on our lives doesn't have to supersede other aspects of our lives with our families.

The same factors that create our legacy, beginning with our spiritual capital, seem also to be the great differentiators between the affluent individuals and families who plan and make big decisions successfully, and those who unintentionally (and sometimes intentionally) "kick the can down the road" factoring only one dimension of what is most important to them into significant decisions. These special factors are also the great differentiators for those individuals and families who have peace and direction even during "storms," and those who feel an internal storm even when their businesses and the economy are going well.

This book is not written from the perspective of a particular religious, spiritual, or philosophical tradition. Although I am of the Christian faith, my research on spiritual capital and wealthy family decision making has allowed me to canvas successful individuals and families from various spiritual traditions and major religions. As a result, only the following two assumptions are made in this book.

- Human beings are both material and spiritual in nature, and these two natures are inextricably linked
- The former nature pulls us toward that which is temporal and the latter nature pulls us toward that which is transcendent

To discover how spiritual capital manifests itself in the lives and work of families, I decided to interview those who were fortunate enough to have an abundance of financial resources. Some of these people became wealthy as a result of creating a very successful company or professional practice, or earning their wealth by working for someone else. Others gained affluence from building on wealth they'd inherited. Ultimately, I came to view them as united by one truth: that spiritual capital is foundational to living and leaving our intended legacy.

I agree with Friedrich Nietzsche, who wrote: "He who has a Why to live for can bear with almost any How."[2] It is important that individual family members have their *whys*—the spiritual capital, or values, purpose, and faith, guiding them—securely in place, and once they do so, that the individual and family, as a collective, is able to succeed on every level.

HOW TO USE THIS BOOK

In a changing world with so many unknowns, spiritual capital is the variable in your life that can ground you and most effectively guide your important family wealth decisions. It is like the GPS system in a car that helps you to navigate life. This book is not intended to provide a linear process to answer the *why* questions for you and your family. I will leave it to you to program the destination that you and your loved ones would like to reach into your own personal decision-making GPS, and name the *whys* behind it. Even so, my intention is that by reading this book and making a personal investment into your spiritual capital you will discover and secure the *whys* needed for you and your family.

These *whys* will be the answers to such questions as:

- "Why should each member of our family have a lasting positive impact in his or her relationships, work, and environment?"
- "Why should I transfer my wealth to future generations?"
- "Why should we not sell the family business?"
- "Why should we select trustees who align with our values and wishes?"
- "Why should I act with love even though the other person has wronged me?"
- "Why should our company's legacy be much more than just making a profit?"
- "Why should I do the right thing even though no one will know otherwise?"
- "Why should I not purchase additional luxuries (even though there isn't anything intrinsically wrong with luxu-

ry) and, instead, give more money to those less materially fortunate than me?"
- "Why should I take a moment to stop and be present with those I live and work with, even though there are a lot of demands on my time?"
- "Why should we not give our son and daughter everything they want, even though we have the resources to do so?"
- "Why should I take the time to care for my mind, body, and spirit?
- "Why should I trust love and not fear?"

Not only is this book designed to help you to address your *whys*, it also explores the *whats* and the *hows* of spiritual capital, and its ability to help you navigate your important family wealth decisions and live your intended legacy.

This book was written to be read as a whole, but you could go to any chapter of particular interest and it would stand on its own. In the two chapters of Part One of this book, I will make the case for the importance of spiritual capital in helping you to navigate the important family wealth decisions in your life, and expand your framework for understanding your wealth. In Part Two, I will then show you a path on how to make the five most important family wealth decisions that impact your legacy.

Throughout this book, I provide evidence for the relevance of incorporating spiritual capital (values, purpose, and faith) into your family's decision making. I have used real case studies from my work (though disguised to protect the privacy of the individuals involved), and anecdotes from my own life. I have interviewed wealthy families and well-known experts so you can hear what they have to say in their own words.

Nonetheless, I admit to you now that the fuller understanding and wisdom that will emerge in your life from reading this book *will only come from your diligent investment in your spiritual capital.* This is so for the same reason that even if I told you why it is important to exercise, and provided the testimonies of others to back this up, you would not experience the benefits until you consistently committed to your own exercise regimen.

I trust that you are about to find your answers, or at least your path to optimizing your five most important family wealth decisions, which will be personally energizing and deeply rewarding to you, your present-day family, and future generations to come. Your decisions will be easier to make, and more importantly, they will be based on what is most important, secure, and lasting to you. Let's take your next step of the journey together and see if we cannot expand on the success you have already experienced in your life.

PART ONE
THE ROAD LESS TRAVELED

"Love is an act of will—namely, both an intention and an action. Will also implies choice. We do not have to love. We choose to love."
—M. Scott Peck

CHAPTER ONE
NAVIGATING YOUR LEGACY

"We are not human beings on a spiritual journey.
We are spiritual beings on a human journey."
—Pierre Teilhard de Chardin

I remember taking family trips as a child. We would all pile into the car and head off. When needed, Dad would have the old, reliable map in hand (or at least in the glove compartment). If the journey was long enough, my parents would identify a hotel to stay at overnight before continuing the journey. It was inevitable that somewhere along the way we would miss a turn. My dad would argue, "It was the map's fault!" This ultimately led to us reluctantly pulling into a gasoline station, miles off course, to ask for directions back to where we were intending to go.

Today, as I prepare for a family trip with my own children, I take out my smartphone, tap on the global positioning system

(GPS) icon, enter my destination, and in seconds I have a detailed course to follow. Not only this, there is a voice telling me ahead of time when to take lefts and rights: "Be prepared to turn in one mile." And if this weren't enough, my GPS app will factor in what can never be known ahead of time when using a paper map: new roads and traffic patterns.

Similarly, when you have to chart a course in your life, such as the course of personal happiness or effectively transferring wealth to your children, you have a choice regarding the technology you will turn to. Will you select the decision-making equivalent of a paper map or of a GPS? Both technologies serve the same purpose: to help you travel from point A to point B. But one is more efficient at getting you the results you want.

Paper roadmaps can help us in our travels, especially those we take by land. But they are one-dimensional in nature and do not actually tell us which roads to travel. If our map is dated and not reflective of a new highway or street, it may send us in the wrong direction, so we never arrive at the destination unless we find another source of information. Despite their limitations, paper maps do provide a tangible benefit in addition to information: They give us a sense of security. We can hold them in our hands and they have been our guides for centuries.

The GPS is clearly a step up in technology from the paper map. It brings the paper map to life and adds multiple dimensions of value. But it does require faith, at least initially, to allow a voice you don't know to tell you which way to go and to trust a route you cannot see (unlike a paper map). I must confess, there has been an occasion or two when I didn't trust the voice and followed what I thought was a better path, thus quickly learning that I should have listened.

GPS technology takes the travel experience to a whole new level. After selecting your intended destination, a course is charted for you, a colorful linear map or topographical map appears on your screen (you get to choose the view you like best), and a voice begins to guide your navigation ("Turn left in 450 feet," "Stay on this road for twenty-one miles," and "You have reached your destination"). It also tells you what time you can expect to arrive at your destination. Not only does the system help you get from point A to point B, it has other, special features, like finding nearby points of interest, gas stations, and hospitals at the touch of a finger.

Having said this, GPS isn't a perfect technology yet, and within the technology there are various levels of effectiveness. I am reminded of a trip I took through Washington, D.C., on my way to Virginia. My DVD-based navigation system had worked wonderfully for much of the journey, only failing me when I arrived at a part of the highway that was undergoing significant construction. (The government was installing a train system from the heart of the Capital to the outlying parts of Virginia.) The GPS told me to get off an exit that wasn't there anymore, and thus it sent me in an endless circle.

Although it is accurate 98 percent of the time, the DVD-based GPS still requires that you keep your eyes open and your brain active, because at the end of the day, you are responsible for making the final call about which way to go.

A satellite receiver is the most basic component of the best version of GPS technology. The receiver on such a system collects and reports data from nearly thirty satellites that orbit the Earth, allowing planes, cars, boats, and individuals to pinpoint their locations practically anywhere on the planet. Although this technology also is not perfect—to work optimally it requires an unobstructed line of sight between the receiver and four or more satellites—it is nonetheless the single most precise and helpful technology that exists at present to navigate a physical journey.

In the best GPS devices, the data from the receiver is updated frequently. The raw data is filtered through the operating software, allowing for the various features the GPS has. In the common DVD-based technology, however, the information received from the satellites orbiting the Earth—the heavens, if you will—is limited by whether or not the software is up to date and how much storage capacity the DVD has. As you likely know, it is important to update your GPS technology regularly (for example, by a trip to the dealer to get the latest mapping software) if it isn't happening automatically.

Just last month I received a flyer from the dealership where I bought my car, stating it was time to update my navigation system. It read: *"Your navigation system is designed to show you the right route to your destination. That can save you time and fuel costs all season long. It can also minimize wear and tear on your vehicle. As roads change, an updated map ensures you're navigating as efficiently as possible. And with the latest map, you'll also discover new points of interest as you drive: restaurants, ATMs, and more."*[1]

It was ironic that I received this flyer while I was writing this chapter. It reminded me that when we have our personal GPS updated and programmed with our values, our purpose, and our faith it minimizes the "wear and tear" on our families, ensures we "navigate" our important decisions more efficiently, and may even lead us to discover "new points of interest" in our lives that we weren't even looking for. We make our best decisions when we allow ourselves to be guided by the things that matter most to us.

What is this equivalent of GPS technology for individual and family wealth decisions to which I am referring? Just ask yourself this: Similar to the GPS voice alerting you to turn left, right or go straight as you take a trip, what voice or voices do you turn to for help in navigating your family wealth decisions? Perhaps the voices of your family, friends, professionals, your intuition, and/or God?

Trust and estate-planning attorneys have provided effective decision-making tools for decades to help their clients focus successfully on the four biggest financial issues, which are taxation, preservation, control, and philanthropy. Financial advisors have similarly leveraged various tools, such as stock selection, asset allocation, and portfolio construction, to help people invest their money. The great news is that for the majority of the cases professional advisers such as these are successful at helping people minimize their taxes, protect their assets, and grow their personal and familial wealth.

All of the aforementioned and related wealth technologies are necessary and valuable when we are ready to make our most important family wealth decisions; however, they have their limitations unless we integrate them with our spiritual technology. They are not able to account for the inevitable transitions that will take place in a family's life: things such as marriages and divorces, illnesses, deaths and births, and the so-called *black swans*, which are statistically improbable events that adversely affect stock markets.[2] Nor do they typically capture the bigger picture regarding the values, purpose, and faith of the larger individual and family legacy. Success at making family wealth decisions has more to do with how the family is prepared for their assets, than the technical side of preparing the assets for the family and investing.

The technology that is needed to optimize the existing wealth decision-making tools is related to the core components of the GPS technology. Similar to the GPS satellite technology, we need to seek out and receive information from a spiritual place via our faith, which functions like the receiver that receives information from the satellites in the orbit. Faith is then integrated with your existing "navigation software" —another name for your values and purpose.

INTEGRATING SPIRITUAL MAPPING INTO YOUR DECISION MAKING

If you accept my premise that you need a *satellite receiver* (faith) integrated with your values and purpose to upgrade your family wealth decision-making technology, then you'll see that the question that needs to be addressed is: *What gives you the greatest perspective or information to help you optimize your most important family wealth decisions?*

My recommendations in this book are not about negating the foundational decision-making technologies of wealth decisions related to tax, law, and finance. Instead, they're about integrating them with the data we receive from our spiritual GPS. We benefit greatly from integrating our values, purpose, and faith into our five most important family wealth decisions. If you're someone who is inner driven to do good in the world for your family, your community, and others who are within your capacity to help, and your desire is to live the legacy you want to leave behind, then navigating every decision you make with the assistance of your spiritual GPS will bring great advantages.

Here is an example of how using the spiritual GPS facilitates decision making and results in a positive living and lasting legacy. I was working closely with the parents of two adult children. The parents already had an estate plan in place, whose overall terms they shared with me. Their plan reflected that their wealth was going to be distributed to their children at three different points in time, determined by the children's ages: age 25, age 30, and age 35.

After learning what the parents valued most and hearing them describe the wishes they had for their children and their beliefs about the purpose of wealth, I quickly realized that their estate plan was unintentionally out of alignment with their intended legacy. The parents said they wanted to preserve their wealth across generations, and also that they wanted their wealth to support their children's passions and well-being. Yet they described their children as having low financial IQs and being somewhat directionless. One child was also struggling with an addiction.

After our conversation, they decided to update their estate plan to better align with their intended family legacy. They decided not to transfer their wealth at those ages. Instead, they would give their children access to assets that would cover their physical and emotional well-being, education, health care needs, and the like, and also to set a plan into motion for raising their financial IQs.

In their new plan, this couple was more intentionally guided by their values and purpose. Given the nature of legacy planning, the process itself actually caused them to reflect upon and reinvest in their spiritual faith.

Spiritual capital is rarely factored into making decisions in our personal and work lives, especially as it pertains to our family wealth decisions, because spirituality is transcendent and relatively intangible, making it harder to trust—at least initially—than more tangible instruments. In the midst of the pragmatic demands of our daily lives, it isn't easy to explain the impact of our spiritual capital or precisely measure it. Anthony Robbins, the famous life coach, doesn't see spirituality as *separate* from everyday decision making and success. Like me, he believes that the process should be fully integrated, a point of view that is reflected in his statement, "To me the notion that spirituality is separate from the rest of life does not allow for a practical approach to living a life that has extraordinary quality."[3]

At this point, you might be thinking, "This doesn't make sense. How can we factor an intangible into our tangible (financial) decisions?" If you haven't yet explored your values, purpose, and faith, it may not make sense, especially if you assume we only have our five senses to leverage to make our most important family wealth decisions. I guess that is why many have referred to a "sixth sense," or intuition, that guides them. Or why Blaise Pascal, a seventeenth-century French philosopher and mathematician, said, "The heart has its reasons that reason knows nothing of."[4] Furthermore, we are not used to relying upon it for planning. Doing so would require us to change from one technology to another (continuing our GPS analogy), and most people like to stick with what they know (the familiar is seductive), even though our spiritual capital makes a powerful impact.

In addition, spiritual faith is rarely openly discussed when financial decisions are being made because conventional wisdom informs us that we are not supposed to talk about politics and religion with anyone outside our circle of close friends and family, and especially not between professionals and their clients. To begin to rely on spiritual capital, you may have to go against this convention, and any internalized taboos.

In this chapter, my aim is to persuade you that it would be beneficial to bring your spiritual GPS up to date—thereby enabling you to receive spiritual insights and wisdom, grounded in what really matters most to you—before making important wealth-related decisions on behalf of yourself or your family. As the late Roy Edward Disney, former senior executive and board member of the Walt Disney Company founded by his uncle, once remarked, "It's not hard to make decisions when you know what your values are."[5]

Remember, the degree to which you do not factor your values, purpose, and faith into your most important family wealth decisions is the exact degree to which your inner GPS cannot help you. It's like disabling or failing to activate the GPS in your car. Navigation requires two inputs: your current position and your destination. Without inputting your values, purpose, and faith into the navigation system of your decisions you could get lost and stray from your path. You might miss the signs that are available to you, and end up going in circles. Your decisions will not be optimized and the imprint you are making on the world—your living and lasting legacy—won't be clear.

Just as importantly as finding your way to achieve your own goals, if you do not program your values, purpose, and faith into your inner GPS you won't be able to help others, such as your children, create their own positive living and lasting legacies. You will be "blind" as a guide.

OUR SPIRITUALITY IS A FORM OF CAPITAL

Spiritus is the Latin word meaning *breath*. The ancient Romans used it to refer to that which breathes vitality into our personal lives and our work. This essence is the divine or transcendent essence of the spiritual navigation systems that guide each of us. Each of us has a spiritual GPS—an inner map of our personal landscape—that includes a unique set of factors and information. It is not for me to tell you what yours is or for you to tell a family member what his or hers is. But it does benefit us all to invest time and energy into building the map, so we have conscious access to its details.

For the purposes of this book, in which we are talking about how spiritual capital shapes and informs the five most important family wealth decisions that impact our legacy (outlined earlier), we will use the same vocabulary to discuss the most tangible capital, like financial capital, with the less tangible capitals, our intellectual, social, human, and spiritual capital, and we will make the assumption that all can be managed through similar processes: via legacy planning.

My intention is to show you that there are interdependent forces at play here, and investing in our spiritual capital is a powerful way to increase the presence of *spiritus* (or perhaps simply our awareness of the presence of *spiritus*) in our personal and work lives—which, of course, is how to optimize your family wealth decisions, and create your desired legacy.

If we were to do a review of the world's major religions and philosophical traditions, it would reveal a common endorsement of a set of core virtues.[6] Along with other perennial philosophical and religious virtues, like wisdom, knowledge, courage, and justice, central to the core virtues recognized by all of these traditions are *spirituality* and *transcendence.* That for millennia so many people and cultures have understood the connection between spiritual capital and the well-being of the individual, the family, and the community is a fact that lends credence to the idea that these core virtues deserve inclusion in our daily affairs in the contemporary world, too.

Do contemporary Americans factor spirituality and core virtues into their work and financial decisions like their forbears did? For the most part, yes. In 2006, the Gallup Organization published the results of a landmark study, *The Spiritual State of the Union,* which revealed that:[7]

- A majority of adults in the United States say the overall health of the nation, including its economic health, depends on the spiritual health of its people.
- A majority thinks of spirituality more in a "personal and individual sense" than in terms of "organized religious and church doctrine."
- Solid majorities of sampled groups say that their religious and spiritual beliefs affect how they invest and save money.[8]
- Among those surveyed who "believe in God," 79 percent said God wants them to work at whatever makes them happiest. Eighty-seven percent said God wants them to

find work that best suits their individual talents. Ninety-one percent held the view that God wants them to do something with their lives that will be useful to the world.

Since I began to perceive the importance of investing in spiritual capital to help navigate the five most important family wealth decisions, and viewing it, alongside a focus on legacy, as one of the hidden keys to their optimization, I have sought out voices of other experts to confirm what I have observed and experienced, not only in my own life, but as a result of working with, and for successful individuals and families for almost the past quarter century. The open conversation about the inclusion of spirituality in the daily lives of Americans has gradually become bolder, even if it's not traditionally expressed.

In a *New York Times* article (December 2011) entitled "Americans: Undecided about God?" Eric Weiner writes:

For a nation of talkers and self-confessors, we are terrible when it comes to talking about God. The discourse has been co-opted by the True Believers, on one hand, and Angry Atheists on the other. What about the rest of us? The rest of us, it turns out, constitute the nation's fastest-growing religious demographic. We are the Nones, the roughly 12 percent of people who say they have no religious affiliation at all. The percentage is even higher among young people; at least a quarter are Nones. Apparently, a growing number of Americans are running from organized religion, but by no means running from God. On average 93 percent of those surveyed say they believe in God or a higher power; this holds true for most Nones—just 7 percent of whom describe themselves as atheists, according to a survey by Trinity College. Nones are the undecided of the religious world. We drift spiritually and dabble in everything from Sufism to Kabbalah to, yes, Catholicism and Judaism.[9]

In a June 2012 *New York Times* article entitled "Buddhists' Delight," James Atlas points out the existence of a new demographic group, whom he refers to as the "Newddhists," a term that describes Westerners hungry for balance, harmony, and a taste of the spiritual who are embracing Buddhism.[10]

We can see from these news reports that spirituality is, at the very least, popular. A major thought leader in the field of family wealth has gone further and asserted the importance of spirituality to family success. In his book *Family Wealth—Keeping It in the Family* (Bloomberg Press, 2004), James E. Hughes, Jr., states:

> *Every family I have observed that is successfully preserving its wealth is a reflection of the five virtues of truth, beauty, goodness, community, and compassion. Transcending all of these is its reflection of love. . . . I am convinced that without this spiritual component, a family cannot succeed in preserving itself.*[11]

Of course, with spiritual capital—the core virtues—being so fundamental to the success of wealthy families, it begs the question: What is a family to do about it? How can we as individuals and family units put our spiritual capital to work for us to optimize our decisions and create our intended legacy? There have been many books written on the technical and structural aspects of legacy planning. There are also plenty of books on spirituality and happiness. But none to date has yet focused exclusively on defining spiritual capital in a way that helps an individual or family do something practical to increase the influence of this transcendent force on its day-to-day affairs and integrating it into legacy planning.

Since helping you optimize your family wealth decisions and create a positive living and lasting legacy is the purpose of my book, I will now share with you my operational definition of spiritual capital through an equation I created.

THE SPIRITUAL CAPITAL EQUATION

Spiritual capital (SC) is the net result of our values (V) plus purpose (P), multiplied by our faith (F). It is a *gestalt* of these variables, which can be understood by the following equation:

$$SC = (V + P) \times F$$

Let's take a moment to define each element in this equation.

Values: Values are core beliefs and important principles, such as family, giving back to the community, and excellence.

Purpose: Purpose refers to the reason for why something is done. For example, to correct injustices or help others make important decisions.

Faith: Faith is the active pursuit, devotion, and metaphysical submission to, and acknowledgment of, a higher power, known by many as the Divine or God (feel free to call it by any name that makes you comfortable). It is the omnipresent dimension of our lives that is not easily seen, touched, or measured, yet is real—not unlike the virtual world of the Internet in which we can interact and engage with one another.

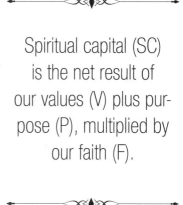

Spiritual capital (SC) is the net result of our values (V) plus purpose (P), multiplied by our faith (F).

We can have established values and purpose, and be doing fairly well with our decisions using those alone, but it is our faith that produces the multiplicative effect of the spiritual capital equation and ultimately optimizes our family wealth decisions. It is through this variable that we can most directly invest into our spiritual nature. Faith-based practices help us transcend the material and mundane aspects of our daily lives, however relevant and necessary these may be.

Deepak Chopra in describing different levels of what he calls "God consciousness" in his book *The Third Jesus* (Three Rivers Press, 2009), says that when we don't pursue spirit, or what I refer to as spiritual capital, there is a "chasm of consciousness."[12] Meaning, without investing in our faith and the non-tangible aspects of our lives, paradoxically we are actually missing out on experiencing the fuller reality of our life and decisions. It is this healthy dialectic between our material and spiritual natures that enables us to optimize our five most important family wealth decisions. When the spiritual is left out of our legacy planning, we can only fall short of our intended living and lasting legacy.

Faith informs and shapes our values and purpose, and ultimately brings them to life. More importantly, faith gives us the perspective and courage to live out our values and purpose in everything we do. This combination produces the wisdom and fuel needed to live out our legacy daily.

We need that fuel! There is value in the simple existence of a car or plane. Some are beautiful to look at, and in a storm they can provide us with shelter. Those are purposes we may find meaningful. But without gasoline to ignite a car or plane's engine, we're not going to be able to drive or fly the vehicle—its highest purpose—and experience the destinations to which it could take us—the true purpose why this vehicle exists. The gasoline of our lives is our spiritual faith.

Human beings are both material and spiritual in nature, and these two aspects of our being are complementary and held in a necessary tension. Our material nature pulls us toward that which is temporal, meaning that we are prone to focus on, and value, that which we can touch, feel, see, and smell, and thereby be able to "prove" exists. Our spiritual nature pulls us toward that which is transcendent, meaning those experiences, intuitions, nudges, gut feelings, and intangible truths that are not easily captured in an Excel spreadsheet, yet could have a profound impact on our daily decisions and intended legacy.

We each have our transcendent moments, those instances that captivate us, help us to think beyond our present circumstances, or experience the Divine. In addition to the more traditional practices of prayer, reflection, and meditation, I have had spiritual moments standing on the beach at dusk holding hands with my wife, watching the opera *La Bohème*, and holding my child soon after birth. As you can plainly see from these examples, both natures feed off the other, but the spiritual nature is the one that, when invested in, gives us the fuel for transcendent guidance or navigation.

When I refer to *transcendence,* I do not mean that we must become ascetics and deny the material world or give away all of our material possessions. Instead, I am suggesting just the *opposite*: that you lean into the material world fully but with the proper perspective, wisdom, and courage to embrace and shape your reality and help you guide your big decisions. It is not about isolation, it is about integration!

The process of legacy planning should begin with the less tangible variables in our lives, such as our values, purpose, and faith. However, while an individual or family absolutely *should* hire a technically competent professional who knows the law, strategies, and techniques of his or her field better than anyone else.

All families need to invest in their spiritual capital, wealthy families especially, since wealth accentuates everything and pulls us magnetically toward a greater focus on temporal issues, like gravity pulls material objects toward the center of the Earth. Simply put, an abundance of financial capital can pull us strongly toward the material side of our human nature. This is nothing to be ashamed of, but it is *very* important that we come to terms with this reality and seek a counter balance. Otherwise, it may unintentionally cause us and our families to make less than ideal decisions that put us out of alignment with our intended legacies—decisions we likely would not have made if we had invested more in our spiritual capital.

KNOWING YOUR *WHY*

Sociologist Paul Schervish, Director of Boston College's Center for Wealth and Philanthropy, in a paper entitled "Receiving and Giving as Spiritual Exercise," says: "When material choice becomes quantitatively abundant, the inner life of desire, aspiration, and want requires education."[13] I believe he is saying that when there is an abundance of financial capital, it is more important to keep it in perspective. Therefore, ongoing investment into our spiritual capital is necessary.

It is a different experience when we quiet the activity and noise in our lives, and the self-centered *me* focus of our egos drops away. We can open up to the transcendent, non-material dimension of our lives through prayer, meditation, and contemplation. When I surveyed my clients, those who invested in the spiritual dimension of their lives by pursuing such practices testified that they were more able to find clarity regarding the decisions they needed to make, to be more patient and empathic, to have the strength not to react in an unconstructive manner, and to have the courage to act on their *calling,* an abiding passion that shapes their lives or a sense of higher purpose. They also were less ego focused, and could delay gratification. In addition, they became clearer about what really matters to them. As a result, their spiritual practices influenced and sometimes reshaped their values and purpose. At the very least, they acknowledged that these spiritual practices ignited their existing values and purposes.

"Okay," you might be saying at this point, "this would be relevant if I were a philosopher, theologian, or a religious person, but I am not. I am a business owner and I live in the real world. I have to make practical decisions every day. What does this mean to me?"

Don't worry, I get it. I am a business owner myself. So let me take my spiritual capital equation and show you the vital importance in business, or could I say, in the *real* world.

I met with new clients, a brother and sister team who had built a very successful family-run business that had the potential to expand rapidly. The reason for the meeting was because they wanted to make sure that any future expansion would not contradict their core business and their respective family values. They referenced the fact that in *Built to Last* (HarperBusiness, 2002) Jim Collins writes in detail about the importance of core values and purpose, and credited his book as having a tremendous impact on their success as a company.[14] Reading his book had inspired them to reach out to me to talk about their intended legacy for their business and respective immediate families.

I asked my clients whether they had yet codified the values that represented the intersection of the business and the family. They informed me that they had done so for the business, but not for the family. When I suggested that they do the same for their family, one responded, "No we have not. How did we miss this? It worked for our business, so it can only help if we integrated it into our family values as well. Thank you!"

I met with them again a couple of months later and they

shared that the suggestion I made not only gave them greater clarity about what was most important to them and the business, but also served them well as an internal compass for the business growth decisions they were about to make. The real beauty of the interaction we'd had from my point of view was that I didn't give them the *whats* or the *hows* of those decisions, I only led them to comprehend the *whys* and then they were able to work out the rest themselves. Being clear on your *whys* is vitally important to answering the hows of your family wealth decisions.

Further reflecting the relevance of knowing your whys, during a TED Talk entitled, "How Great Leaders Inspire Action," Simon Sinek states that based on his research, great leaders and successful companies start by answering the *why* questions in their lives, or what I would refer to as the *purpose* question, not the *what* or *how,* which is a more conventional leadership approach. In describing the why question, Sinek states, "What is your cause, your purpose, your belief? Why does your organization exist and why should anyone care?"[15] Knowing your answers to these types of questions will help you better navigate your important family wealth decisions.

On a similar note, in the business book *The E-Myth Revisited* (HarperBusiness, 1995), Michael Gerber states:

> *Something is missing in most of our lives. Part of what is missing is purpose. Values. Worthwhile standards against which our lives can be measured. . . .*
>
> *In a world without purpose, without meaningful values, what have we to share but our emptiness, the needy fragments of our superficial selves?*
>
> *As a result, most of us scramble about hungrily seeking distraction, in music, in television, in people, in drugs. . . .*

What most people need, then, is a place of community that has purpose, order and meaning.[16]

Later, Gerber goes on to say:

I know that my spirit is waiting out there in front of me on one of any number of paths, and that it's up to me to choose that one path on which my spirit waits, and to step out on it brightly, without hesitation, to pursue the I, which is the greatest one I can possibly be. To be spirit-full, that is spiritual. That is to be in touch with my soul.[17]

Although Gerber does not refer to spiritual capital in a book that has sold over one million copies, and which was written for small businesses, he spelled out in his own words my spiritual capital equation [SC = (V + P) x F] and its vital importance in our work lives.

To illustrate how key spiritual capital is to optimizing your family wealth decisions, I want to introduce you to another family that I worked with. This particular family had recently experienced two significant events in their lives: a loss of a family member and a significant expansion of their liquidity resulting from the loss. It is not hard to imagine that they had a range of mixed feelings about what to do with their newfound financial capital, and questions that ranged from "What are we to do with this new liquid money?" to "How shall we go on without Mitchell?"

We addressed various aspects of their lives ranging from their finances to how they would move forward together. One of the results of our work together was in essence to create their mission statement. The following statements reflect what they agreed upon.

- "Our family is committed to maintaining loving and close family relationships across the generations. This closeness allows and respects individual differences and preferences, yet we understand we may need to keep our individual preferences in check from time to time for the greater good of the family."
- "As a family, we value a full life based on all our family capitals. Our financial capital will always serve the vision of our family and never the other way around."
- "We believe we are stewards of our family capitals and strongly believe in sharing our resources to better the lives of others and sustain the environment."

Their family's mission statement enabled them over the next twelve months to make successful decisions regarding what leadership role each adult family member would play to ensure family success (for instance, one was put in charge of giving, and another was put in charge of identifying an appropriate estate planning team), how best to structure their shared assets, and how much and to which charities they would direct their combined giving. They were very satisfied with the result and through the process felt they became much closer. By answering their *why* first, they were able to answer other important questions.

I also want to share with you a particular example of the type of results that the continued investment into my own spiritual capital has manifested at the intersection of my personal and professional life. I trust that you have your own version of needing to make an important decision that could impact your legacy, or maybe it is someone like an adult child who is at a point in his life where he must decide if his professional goals are beneficial for his immediate family.

For many years, I had a successful career inside of global

corporate institutions. I worked with interesting, diverse, and successful people, and traveled to countries around the globe as part of my work. Originally, getting in a plane to go work in Switzerland, Hong Kong, or Dubai was exciting, but during the final couple of years in this position any travel felt taxing to me, and it took me away from my wife and children. I found it increasingly harder to be creative and innovative. It wasn't like anything was going wrong. Actually, everything was going well . . . on paper. Even in my family life, things were going great. But I had started to reassess what was my intended legacy, what I believed my purpose should be going forward, and whether I believed God was calling me to do something else.

The investment I made into my spiritual capital led me to a decision point, the aforementioned intersection: Would I stay in my secure, successful career or launch out on my own and build my own company?

I must confess that I was equally excited and nervous at the thought of going out on my own. *Why would I leave my job when all is going well on the surface?* I wondered. *Why would I go from bringing in a secure, successful income to not knowing when I will get paid again? And is this the time to do it, with children depending on me for their financial well-being?*

Well, you know where this story is going. I sought advice from those I trusted (including an executive life coach), was diligent in my preparation, and prayed a lot. And yes, when I was honest with myself and my wife, it was time to step out in faith and go after my calling. So I did. In short, the decision I made, which could have gone either way, was definitely the best decision. Since starting my business, I am more fully aligned with my values and purpose, and my creative energy is overflowing. I am more integrated into my family's daily life (which is one of my highest values) and feel excited to be building a business around my calling. Daily, I feel I am closer to living out my legacy because I was able to optimize my decision by leveraging my spiritual capital.

My family's journey is not over yet, because I know that there will be other important decision points along the way, but the investment we have made into our spiritual capital has further prepared me and my wife for the next inevitable decisions that will come our way.

I trust that you are beginning to see how important values, purpose, and faith are in optimizing your five most important family wealth decisions. Maybe you are at a decision point of some kind in your own professional or personal life—an intersection—and not sure which way to turn? Maybe you are trying to help someone you love make an important decision? Or maybe you are ready to start or update your legacy planning? If so, then, I invite you to consider the question: *Which technology will I choose?*

Will you stick with what you know (the equivalent of a paper map) or take the time to program your inner, spiritual GPS with your values, purpose, and faith?

As we travel together through the balance of chapters in this book, your path will get clearer and you may even find points of interest along the way that you and your family weren't expecting.

Buckle up, sit back, and enjoy your journey.

CHAPTER TWO

PREPARING FOR YOUR LEGACY JOURNEY

*"Everything that can be counted does not necessarily count;
everything that counts cannot necessarily be counted."*
—Sir George Pickering, as quoted by Albert Einstein

One of the part-time jobs I had during my college years was driving a school bus. It was a great way to earn a few dollars and yet have plenty of time remaining for my studies. I would pick up the students in the early morning and take them back home at the end of the day, allowing me the time between and after to attend classes and study. Or sometimes I would take them on a school trip. I would drive them to a destination, such as a museum, and then wait in the bus until they reemerged to be taken back to school. The waiting period allowed me to focus on my studies.

There was one thing that had to take place before any of

these trips happened: going through a pre-trip checklist. There were a number of items on the bus that I needed to make sure were properly functioning before departure, some inside the bus and others outside the bus. Pilots have a comparable version of a pre-trip checklist they use before flying their planes.

Unlike the bus driver or pilot examples, most of us don't review a pre-trip checklist each and every time we get in our automobiles to go somewhere. Somehow we trust that everything will function just fine and we will safely arrive at our destination. Nevertheless, we do have to bring our vehicles into the garage from time-to-time for service (such as getting an oil change or having the tires rotated), and depending on where we live, we must have our cars thoroughly inspected by a certified third party every year or two. We do not check the oil, air pressure in the tires, or necessarily ensure that we have plenty of gasoline when we are just taking a ride to the local food mart to pick up milk or bread. However, if we are planning a long trip, especially to a destination we haven't traveled to before, we do tend to have our own customized version of a pre-trip checklist. For example, we check that there is a full tank of gas, snacks, and books on CD.

Similarly, when we take longer-type "trips" in our lives, such as marriage, having children, and making important family wealth decisions that impact our legacies, it is important that we develop an appropriate pre-trip checklist. When it comes to individual and family wealth, we all too often focus on checking only one dimension of our wealth—that is our financial capital—whereas the list really should include a review of every type of capital we possess.

If you ask someone the following question, "What is your net worth?" nine times out of ten you will get some type of numerical response, such as, "Around one million, if you factor in our home," "Twenty million, not including the company," or "Just north of three hundred million." If I were to ask you the same question, "What is your net worth?" how would you respond?

Knowing your financial net worth, or if you own a family business the financial worth of the business, is *very* relevant and important. Such information is the foundation of what enables all of us to meet our basic needs and provide opportunities for those around us and future generations; invest into our companies to provide greater value to economies around the world, thereby providing jobs to hundreds and thousands of people; and giving back to society in significant ways via faith-based institutions and charities, for example. The traditional way to access this information is by looking at your individual or family's net worth or income statement, and the balance sheet or statement of financial position of your business.

Yet, as we've already seen, there are other capitals that individuals and families have on their *balance sheets* that are rarely considered when we think of an individual's or a family's net worth, or a company's financial worth. Like on the pre-trip checklist for driving the school bus, there are aspects of the balance sheet that we should all check along the way that are internal and external to us. Only by carefully considering these less tangible capitals will a clear vision of our true net worth, the optimization of our five most important family wealth decisions, and our intended legacy be realized.

Clearly financial capital is the easiest to count out of all the family capitals. Yet, we must re-

> Focusing only on our financial capital during our legacy planning limits our effectiveness in some areas of our lives that matter greatly to most of us.

mind ourselves that although the other capitals, especially spiritual capital, aren't as easy *to count*, they are a more complete way to understand our true net worth.

Focusing only on our financial capital during our legacy planning limits our effectiveness in some areas of our lives that matter greatly to most of us. For instance, it does *not* ensure that:

- Our financial wealth will successfully transfer beyond the second and third generations.
- Future generations will be prepared to steward and grow their financial wealth.
- Our family members will have vibrant and close relationships.
- We will maximize the giving and sharing of our resources with others.
- We will have true happiness, purpose, and ultimate net worth.

Also, as the eighth-century Chinese Zen master Hsi-Tang said, "Although gold dust is precious, when it gets in your eyes, it obstructs your vision."[1]

A BROADER UNDERSTANDING OF OUR NET WORTH: THE FISHS FRAMEWORK

To gain an accurate understanding of the wealth and worth of an individual, a family, or a family business, it is helpful to employ the FISHS framework to look at elements from the five capitals we've been discussing: the financial, intellectual, social, human, and spiritual (FISHS) capitals. The following descriptions show how different types of capital assets are manifested, along with a few examples of how they can be worked with on occasion.

FINANCIAL CAPITAL

Recently, I was talking with my clients, Jay and Margaret, about their financial picture. As they described their financial wealth, they described the stock they had in a retail company that was started by Margaret's parents, the present value of their operating company, their homes, the investments they had in various annuities and bonds, and the cash they were purposely keeping out of the markets. The assets they referenced and others, such as annuities, mutual funds, alternative investments, jewelry, collectibles, planes, boats, and art, are all examples of a family's financial capital. In a broader sense, anything you would find on a conventional net worth statement or balance sheet that is considered an asset, liability, and/or ownership equity, is considered financial capital.

Related to, yet different from financial capital, are the wealth structures used to properly secure the financial capital and enable the wishes of prior and existing generations to carry forth to some future point in time. For example, wills and trusts, insurance policies, and other legal entities.

INTELLECTUAL CAPITAL

Intellectual capital manifests itself in various ways. For example, it could be the formal education of your family members, or the experiential knowledge and wisdom they accumulate by going through challenging times. These assets would include the knowledge and wisdom gained from trusting your gut instincts and making big "bets" to start what is now a successful family business, but at one time was just an idea. In addition, the knowledge attained from reading books, doing research on the Internet, having an expertise in a certain region or marketplace, emotional intelligence, and intellectual property are examples of intellectual capital.

One of the families I was working with was in the third generation of a family business. During one of their family meetings, the youngest generation was providing a business update to the larger family. And what they acknowledged was that the intellectual capital they had, which was the basis of the success of their company, might not be what would be needed in the future given the shifts in the marketplace and in government legislation. So they began a strategic business planning process to "put their heads together" to adapt and stay ahead of the curve.

SOCIAL CAPITAL

When I work with families it is common for their other trusted advisors to be fully integrated into my process. In many cases, they will bring me into their processes as well. During one family meeting, I was at the table listening to a discussion between a family and their estate attorney. I heard them mention the names of their trustees and other individuals in the community with whom they had relationships, including nationally recognized people. Wealth, especially significant wealth, frequently creates access to public figures; local, national, and international experts; and executive leaders in organizations.

Social capital refers to the network of relationships we have inside and outside the family, and just as importantly, the quality of these relationships. Particular forms of social capital manifest in membership on the boards we sit on; the people and organizations with whom we volunteer our resources of time, talent, and treasure; and in the relationships we develop in our personal lives, with friends and family, and our professional lives, with co-workers, colleagues, customers, employees, and trusted advisors.

This network of social relationships provides us with very important resources, access, knowledge, and from time to time support and wisdom as we navigate the transitions of our lives.

It also provides us with an opportunity to express our values by giving back and connecting to our higher purpose.

HUMAN CAPITAL

Human capital refers to the values, passions, likes, interest, gifts, and internal "wiring" of each person. It's not only about what we contribute or how productive we are, but also about what makes us tick, gives us energy, how we deploy our energy, and what excites us about living. When evaluating these assets, it is important to go beyond looking at people in terms of their demographics and integrate their psychographics into the picture.

Similar to the one-dimensional response you typically get when asking people about their net worth, it's also not uncommon to pigeonhole human capital into a simple calculation of what people are skilled at, or how productive they are, or are not. A job title is sometimes used to capture a snapshot of this type of capital—for example, "Seiko is head of the marketing division." Typically we ask, "So, Seiko, what do you do?" We rarely ask, "So, Seiko, tell me about who you are?" though the latter question would expand our insights.

Human capital optimally incorporates the holistic health of each person. It is important to understand the potential for predisposed illnesses or the longevity of life in prior generations. This understanding enables us to be proactive in ensuring a well-rounded health and lifestyle plan.

SPIRITUAL CAPITAL

To reiterate, spiritual capital is defined as the net result of our values, purpose, and spiritual faith. It is the gestalt of these variables. When others have written about spiritual capital, they typically positioned it as part of the human capital or social capital assets, and described it as somewhat synonymous with values. I do not believe that spiritual capital is synonymous with values even though it has a direct relationship to them. Spiritual faith (an important variable in my spiritual capital equation) in fact informs our values, shapes our purpose, and most importantly, gives us the courage and strength to live them out. Also, we may have core values of which none is spirituality. So this definition of spiritual capital includes values that are found under human capital.

Explaining the relationship between spiritual capital and social capital, yet reflecting their distinctions, Theodore Roosevelt Malloch, in his book *Spiritual Enterprise: Doing Virtuous Business* (Encounter Books, 2008), appropriately states:

> *But spiritual capital, while it feeds into the process and provides it with an invaluable underpinning* [referring to social capital—author], *it is built up in another way. It comes from another relation altogether than the relations of human society: the relation with God. The reaching out towards God through worship, prayer, devotion and pious observance is a specific kind of discipline, which is not the discipline of human society. It involves an act of metaphysical submission, a bowing down of the whole spirit to a power that lies beyond the world of our perception.*[2]

One of the families I have been working with for a number of years not only begins each of their family meetings in prayer, but has acknowledged that their family mission is to honor God in their family and business. One of the family members told me, "Our family wealth enables us to do what we ought to do."

If you were asked the question "What ought you to do?" how would you answer it?

For the purposes of the individual or family capital balance sheet, the following are examples of *spiritual assets.*

- Various religious or spiritual traditions, including both those that have been passed down from prior generations and those that were recently established
- Various spiritual practices, such as prayer, reflection, contemplation, and meditation
- Experiences of faith
- Associations with, and memberships in faith-based institutions
- Faith in a higher power
- Shared faith with significant others
- Demonstrations of love to self, others, and society at large
- Good works
- State of contentment
- Trust in a greater purpose
- A purposeful life
- Living a virtuous life

I use the FISHS framework to help people broaden their understanding of their true wealth and resources. For example, my clients complete a worksheet known as the Family Capitals Balance Sheet. Each respective family unit completes this document and brings it to their family meeting. During the family meeting, each in turn reads the assets his or her respective family has listed for the five capitals and then together everyone rolls them into one combined Family Capitals Balance Sheet. For subsequent annual family meetings, they update their Family Capitals Balance Sheet together.

Through doing this exercise, one family realized that across the ranks of their large multigenerational family (social capital) they had a number of highly educated educators (intellectual capital), and yet had never thought until then of leveraging this asset for other members of the family. As a result, they decided to set up a more formal way to prepare the next generation (human capital) by utilizing the talents of those family members.

AN INITIAL ASSESSMENT: THE TEN FISHS QUESTIONS

Now you try the exercise. Take a few minutes to answer the following ten questions to gauge how important each of the capitals are to you and your family. On a scale from 1–5, where 1 means it is not important at all, and 5 means it is of the utmost important, to what extent is each question important to you (and your family as a whole)? Circle your answers.

You can also get a downloadable version of this exercise online by visiting: LegacyCapitals.com/resources.

FINANCIAL CAPITAL

1. How important is it to have a clear plan to ensure the success of your family's financial assets (capital) over time?

$$1 \qquad 2 \qquad 3 \qquad 4 \qquad 5$$

2. How important is it to have a clear plan to transfer your financial assets to future generations?

$$1 \qquad 2 \qquad 3 \qquad 4 \qquad 5$$

3. How important is it to have a clear plan to financially give back to the people and organizations that represent your values?

$$1 \qquad 2 \qquad 3 \qquad 4 \qquad 5$$

INTELLECTUAL CAPITAL

4. How important is it to ensure that your family and/or company invest into education, professional development, and lifelong learning?

1   2   3   4   5

SOCIAL CAPITAL

5. How important is it to have your family members volunteer their time and talents to the community and world via boards, charitable institutions, and the like?

1   2   3   4   5

HUMAN CAPITAL

6. How important is it to fully understand the gifts, personalities, passions, and talents of all family members and/or employees?

1   2   3   4   5

7. How important is it to have a clear set of shared family values to govern how all major decisions are made for your family and/or family business?

1   2   3   4   5

SPIRITUAL CAPITAL

8. How important is it to ensure that your family goes beyond financial success and reaches significance?

1   2   3   4   5

9. How important is it that your family has some type of spiritual foundation?

1   2   3   4   5

10. How important is it that your family is an active participant in some type of faith-based institution that reflects your spiritual beliefs?

1   2   3   4   5

I trust the preceding questions have helped you assess what matters most to you and your family at this time, and provided you with a broader framework to make future investment decisions in your various family capitals. Ultimately, I believe you'll see for yourself how your spiritual capital is your life's GPS, helping you to navigate the investment in, and deployment of, your other capitals. When a family is clear on its values and purpose and invests in their spiritual faith, they have the necessary roadmap and "fuel" to optimize the five most important family wealth decisions that contribute to their legacy.

Having said this, investing in your spiritual capital is an ever-evolving process. Similar to a GPS in your phone, car, plane, or boat, there will be times you need to course correct due to "traffic" or "turbulence," like personal conflicts or business failures, or if you run into unforeseen variables like a "new road" or "fast-approaching storms" that aren't yet reflected in your GPS software—anything from spouses joining the family, to divorces, the birth of grandchildren, and serious illnesses. This is an evolutionary principle. Just as Charles Darwin and other biologists have showed us, it is not the strongest or even the most intelligent member of a species that survives and thrives, but the one that is most adaptable to change.[3] The ultimate family wealth GPS can help your family adapt no matter what conditions you encounter in the future.

YOUR PRE-TRIP CHECKLIST

Before you move forward in your legacy planning, as part of your pre-trip checklist, make sure you have your *whys, whats,* and *hows* securely in place. Remember what Friedrich Nietzsche said: "He who has a Why to live for can bear with almost any How."[4]

In each of the chapters in Part Two we will talk about the importance of spiritual capital, however, it is assumed that only *you* can determine the *whys* behind your decisions. So to help secure your *whys, whats,* and *hows,* spend some time reflecting upon the following three questions.

- "What are my core values?"
- "What is the purpose of my life and work?"
- "What is the technology that allows me to tap into transcendent guidance and wisdom?"

In addition, based on your five capitals, assess your level of investment into each respective capital. Are you under invested, somewhat invested, or fully invested?

Based on your self-assessment, you may decide to further invest in a particular capital, knowing that doing so will help in optimizing your family wealth decisions and living out your intended legacy. Circle your responses.

FINANCIAL CAPITAL: "I AM . . ."

Under invested   Somewhat invested   Fully invested

INTELLECTUAL CAPITAL: "I AM . . ."

Under invested   Somewhat invested   Fully invested

SOCIAL CAPITAL: "I AM . . ."

Under invested   Somewhat invested   Fully invested

HUMAN CAPITAL: "I AM . . ."

Under invested   Somewhat invested   Fully invested

SPIRITUAL CAPITAL: "I AM . . ."

Under invested   Somewhat invested   Fully invested

Now that you have prepared your pre-trip checklist, let's begin your legacy planning.

PART TWO

LANDMARKS ON YOUR FAMILY WEALTH JOURNEY

"The choices we make about the lives we live determine the kinds of legacies we leave."
—Tavis Smiley

CHAPTER THREE

THE PURSUIT OF HAPPINESS

"You are not your income. Discover your true worth by letting money serve its purpose as you seek out yours."
—Anonymous

It was a lovely spring day as Michelle and I talked about her life and work. Michelle was in her late twenties, single, and a graduate of a top university. She had a couple of close friends, had lost her father a few years back, and was very close with her mother and two sisters. She described her family as "wealthy" and told me that her parents and grandparents had built a company that enabled their family to want for nothing. Michelle came to me for coaching, as although there was nothing really wrong in her life, she felt like something was missing. I asked what her goal was for our coaching work together. She said, "I just want to be happy."

It was about 6:50 P.M., ten minutes before my scheduled dinner appointment with Himanshu and Nanda. Himanshu and Nanda where planning to sell their business in the near future and as a result were expecting a meaningful amount of liquid wealth. They were both raised in what they described as "middle class" families. As part of their planning for this anticipated event, to their credit, they wanted to ensure their impending wealth did not have a negative effect on their fourteen-year old daughter and twelve-year old son. Just a few minutes after 7:00 P.M. I saw Himanshu and Nanda approaching the table I had reserved for us. We greeted each other, ordered from the menu, and continued the conversation that was started on the phone a couple of weeks prior.

Himanshu said, "I have mixed feelings about the sale. I look forward to having the money to take care of my family and we will finally go on a well-deserved vacation. My one concern is that, although the folks who are buying our company said they will take care of our employees, you just never know."

Nanda added, "We are both concerned that the amount of money we are expecting can have a negative impact on our children."

I asked, "What do you mean by a negative impact?"

She said, "I don't want our children to be spoiled or to have the same entitlement mentality I have seen in other children who come from wealthy families. I don't want them to lose the middle-class values that Himanshu and I were raised with."

I then asked, "It is clear what you don't want to happen to your children, so what impact do you want the wealth to have on your children?"

And they both said, almost in harmony, "I want them to be happy!"

It was early July, during the offseason, when a wealth manager introduced me to his client Darren, a professional athlete. Darren's wealth manager wanted me to work with him because,

"Darren isn't making good choices in his personal life." Even though Darren was on the backend of the typical life span of a professional athlete, he was still earning a significant amount of money through his contract and endorsements. During our conversations Darren shared with me that even though he had "partied hard" for years, enjoyed his share of women, and purchased numerous luxury items, he was beginning to think about what happens when his career as a professional athlete was over. He then added, "No one would know this, but when I am alone and there are no cameras around, I am not really that happy."

Maybe Aristotle was correct when he said, "Happiness is the meaning and the purpose of life, the whole aim and end of human existence."[1] Whether working with a third-generation family member, a patriarch and matriarch anticipating sudden wealth, or a professional athlete whose career is winding down, it is very common that this is one of their primary goals. James Hughes, in his book *Family Wealth*, contends, "While I believe the purpose of a family is to enhance the pursuit of happiness of its individual members, and thereby preserve its human, intellectual, and financial capital, each family must determine and define its philosophy for itself."[2] Both these statements beg the questions, "What is happiness?" and, "How is it achieved?"

How you define your pursuit of happiness is one of the top five most important family wealth decisions and it is at the core of living a positive legacy every day. Happiness has everything to do with your internal sense of being and how others experience you. And, as will be evidenced in the subsequent chapters, it is a key that's critical to being able to answer other impactful questions pertaining to transferring wealth and next-generation preparation.

It is very important for us to remember that money really is just a tool. Although it comes to be a symbol of many other

> If we believe that the sole purpose of money is to bring us happiness, we can only be let down.

things in our lives (for example, power, security, freedom), at its essence, money is neutral. It is we who define its purpose and meaning in our lives. And depending upon how we define its purpose, we find ourselves and the ones we love on a continuum that at one end reflects great despair, somewhere in the middle, short-lived happiness, and at the other end, lasting, passionate, and fulfilled lives. If we believe that the sole purpose of money is to bring us happiness, we can only be let down. However, if we believe that money is to serve our purpose, then it will only enhance our happiness. Shortly, I will provide other attributes that contribute to happiness.

Intentionally or unintentionally defining our purpose as the pursuit of material wealth, as well as focusing exclusively on our financial capital during our legacy planning, can only cause us to fall short of optimizing our family wealth decisions and living out our intended legacy.

That's why finding our purpose is at the heart of our spiritual capital decision-making equation: $SC = (V + P) \times F$. It's also why decisions guided by spiritual capital do lead to lasting happiness. I will now explain the proper understanding of how money can enhance our happiness.

MONEY AND THE PURSUIT OF HAPPINESS

A number of years ago I took a trip to visit the Grand Canyon. I can still remember vividly turning down one of the roads toward the canyon and getting my first glimpse of its magnificent beauty.

If you've been there, you may have shared a similar experience. It is awesome, and if I may say so, it was a spiritual experience. My desire was to get closer and take it all in. After I checked into the hotel, I took a hike down into the canyon, where, to my surprise, my heightened sense of expectation gave way to disappointment. The closer I got to it, the more the canyon lost its majesty. Figuratively speaking, I "got too close to it" and was no longer able to appreciate its full beauty.

The same phenomenon applies to our relationship with our financial capital. It is paradoxical. The closer we get to it, the less significance it seems to have. The closer we personally associate our happiness to money, the more it loses its value and the less happy we are. Like the Buddha said, "Money is like water, try to grab it and it flows away, open your hands and it will move towards you."[3]

Similarly, by taking the words out of context, some people mistakenly believe that when Jesus said, "For the love of money is the root of all kinds of evil" (1 Timothy 6:10), this verse means that money is intrinsically evil. In fact, Jesus is saying the *love* of money for its own sake causes problems, not having an abundance of money in and of itself.

The more financial abundance we have, the more we are potentially pulled toward our material nature. Which is why it is critically important to be fully invested in our spiritual capital. It ensures that we are able to keep a proper perspective on money's purpose in our lives.

When we look to our financial capital alone to bring us lasting happiness, we often encounter disappointment, and even, in some cases, deep despair. When a person has the means to do anything and yet lacks personal confidence in who he is, or lacks purpose in his life, then despair is almost inevitable. Research suggests that money has no correlation to lasting happiness when a person earns above $50,000–$75,000 dollars annually. In other words, whether a person goes to work and earns $100,000 dollars or $100 million dollars annually, neither scenario ensures lasting happiness. A phenomenon regarding the accumulation of, and *pursuit* of money has been captured in the term *affluenza*, which sometimes is referred to as *the rich person's disease.* Some of the symptoms are loss of motivation, low self-esteem, inability to delay gratification, and a sense of entitlement. At a certain point continuing to amass wealth for its own sake does not help us personally flourish nor does it enhance our intended legacy. Furthermore, the potential for affluenza is one of the greatest fears wealth holders have when contemplating transferring wealth to their children, and when deciding whether or not to talk with their children and grandchildren about the level of financial capital that is present in their families.

There is now a new branch of psychology, called *positive psychology,* pioneered by Martin Seligman and Mihaly Csikszentmihalyi, which studies happiness. Traditionally, psychology has focused on how to treat psychological problems, but positive psychology looks at how we can become happier and more fulfilled.

In his book, *Authentic Happiness,* Seligman writes: "How important money is to you, more than money itself, influences your happiness. Materialism seems to be counterproductive: at all levels of real income, people who value money more than other goals are less satisfied with their income and with their lives as a whole."[4]

If wealth alone could bring us deep meaning and happiness, then there would be a strong positive correlation between wealth and happiness, and the most affluent people in the world would be the happiest. But it is self-evident that this correlation does not always exist. *The Atlantic* magazine published an article in early 2011 entitled "Secret Fears of the Super-Rich," citing an unpublished Boston College study of the super-rich that loudly echoes this truth. This study surveyed 165 households with an average net worth of $78 million dollars and 120 households exceeding $25 million.[5] In the article, contributing editor Graeme Wood reports:

The result is a surprising litany of anxieties: their sense of isolation, their worries about work and love, and most of all, their fears for their children. . . . But the overwhelming concern of the super-rich—mentioned by nearly every parent who participated in the survey—is their children. Many express relief that their kids' education was assured, but are concerned that money might rob them of ambition. Having money "runs the danger of giving them a perverted view of the world," one respondent writes. Another worries, "Money could mess them up—give them a sense of entitlement, prevent them from developing a strong sense of empathy and compassion."[6]

Old Testament literature is ripe with illustrations of the limited role money plays in our happiness. Consider King Solomon's words in Ecclesiastes (2:3–11). He is presented as the quintessential prototype of success, a man with great wisdom, power, and money. He says:

I wanted to see what was good for people to do under the heavens during the few days of their lives. I undertook great projects: I built houses for myself and planted vineyards. I made gardens and parks and planted all kinds of fruit trees in them. I made reservoirs to water groves of flourishing trees. I bought male and female slaves and had other slaves who were born in my house. I also owned more herds and flocks than anyone in Jerusalem before me. I amassed silver and gold for myself, and the treasure of kings and provinces. I acquired male and female singers, and a harem as well—the delights of a man's heart. I became greater by far than anyone in Jerusalem before me. In all this my wisdom stayed with me. I denied myself nothing my eyes desired; I refused my heart no pleasure. My heart took delight in all my labor, and this was the reward for all my toil. Yet when I surveyed all that my hands had done and what I had toiled to achieve, everything was meaningless, a chasing after the wind; nothing was gained under the sun.[7]

Notice the ending phrase: "under the sun." This refers to everything outside heaven, meaning that which is not grounded in the spiritual nature of humanity. After pursuing and experiencing all kinds of pleasures and material blessings, Solomon concludes that it was like "chasing after the wind." When only focusing on the non-spiritual forms of capital, especially in a materialistic way as Solomon did, it is hard for us to achieve lasting happiness.

Another subtler factor that reflects the limited role our financial capital has on our lasting happiness is what is referred to by some as the "hedonic treadmill." We fairly quickly adapt to material possessions we've acquired. Expectations rise as a result of gaining anything, whether it is money or objects, so that which once brought us some sense of happiness in the past no longer has the same impact, and possessions are actually taken for granted.

I have seen this phenomenon play out in my own life. A few years back, while interacting with our children during the holiday season, my wife and I spent weeks shopping and gift wrapping, getting ready for Christmas morning. Christmas Eve came and the grandparents arrived bringing many gifts, which our children got to open before Christmas morning. All the other gifts were placed around the tree. We finally went to bed (so we wouldn't get in the way of Santa Claus) and then, before we knew it, the children were shaking us to wake up and go downstairs. There was a flurry of energy, wrapping paper was torn and thrown all over the room. Clothes, toys, and gadgets were lying around everywhere. When the smoke cleared, there may have been one Spider-Man doll in the hand of our youngest and our other children were saying, "I am hungry, can we please have breakfast?" One of them even blurted out, "Is that it?"

Since then, my wife and I not only have reduced the number of gifts we give at Christmas, we have also spent more time with our children serving other families in need at the holidays and throughout the year, and more overtly modeling an attitude of gratefulness for what we do have.

On a related note, I have been in too many conversations with patriarchs and matriarchs sitting in their luxurious homes with views that many other people go on vacations to see, listening to them tell tales of their broken hearts regarding how they wished they were closer to one or more of their children or how they wished their children were closer with each other. Often they say they wish their children appreciated what they had been given and didn't have such an entitlement mentality. Unintentionally, money became the language with which these people expressed love and attempted to "buy" happiness within their families. Now left with emptiness and dissatisfaction, they regret the family legacy they had hoped for hadn't yet been realized. So, if money doesn't ensure our happiness, then what does? How can we achieve it? How do we not "chase after the wind"?

HAPPINESS AND POSITIVE PSYCHOLOGY

There is a growing body of research in the field of positive psychology on the attributes that contribute to lasting happiness and personal well-being. Positive psychology has flipped on its head the traditional line of questions that the field of psychology asked for decades, from "How do we make depressed or sick people feel less depressed and sick?" to "What are the attributes of those who experience true happiness and personal well-being that others should emulate?"

There are various individuals and institutions involved in happiness research. As previously mentioned, Martin E.P. Seligman, Ph.D., from the University of Pennsylvania has discovered that lasting happiness is traceable to having a meaningful and purposeful life, as defined by using our strengths and resources in the service of something greater than ourselves. Seligman refers to this type of life as the *meaningful life*.[8] By contrast, his research has shown that simply striving after positive emotions, or in other words shortcuts to happiness, leaves us empty and ultimately unfulfilled. In his book *Flourish* (Free Press, 2011), he adds *accomplishment* and *positive personal relationships* to his definition of authentic happiness or what he reframes in this book as well-being.[9]

As a result of surveying the resources on happiness, as well as from my own life's research, here is a summary of some of the core attributes associated with authentic happiness. Each of these is an aspect of a person's living legacy, too, as these attributes are central ways we positively impact people's lives and the world.

- Giving back/sharing with others
- Finding our purpose and meaning
- Cherishing relationships

- Being grateful
- Practicing forgiveness (toward ourselves and others)
- Being playful
- Being open
- Being true to ourselves
- Achieving worthwhile goals
- Having faith

These are not only the attributes associated with lasting happiness and well-being; they are also skills to be practiced in our daily lives. For example, daily I try to make time to reflect on the blessings and challenges in my life and am thankful for them. Yes, you read that correctly, I am thankful for the challenges in my life. I might not like the feelings associated with challenges, however I have learned to view them as opportunities to enhance my living legacy.

Dr. Seligman, who acknowledges wavering between atheism and agnosticism, writes, "The relation of hope for the future and religious faith is probably the cornerstone of why faith so effectively fights despair and increases happiness."[10] Hope for the future is an aspect of legacy.

The attribute of giving back or sharing with others was a theme common to many of the resources I surveyed. One international study conducted by social scientist Michael I. Norton, Ph.D., an associate professor at Harvard Business School, found that, in almost every country around the world, when people have the choice to spend money on themselves or on someone else, if they choose someone else they are happier.[11]

Maybe you are saying to yourself, "This is interesting, however research and books do not represent real life." Okay, fair enough, so allow me to share with you what billionaires think about this topic. One would think those who have reached the billionaire level would know whether or not they were happy, or how much their financial capital contributes to their happiness. In October 28, 2011, the television show *20/20* aired an episode entitled "Billionaire Secrets: What They Know That Can Change Your Life."[12] Here is some of what they shared with us (italics added).

- Figure out what you're so passionate about that you'd be *happy* doing it for ten years, even if you never made any money from it. Then do that.
- Always be *true to yourself.*
- Figure out what your *values* are and then live by them in business and in life.
- Rather than focus on work-life separation, focus on *work-life integration.*
- Don't network. Focus on *building real relationships* and friendships where the relationship itself is its own reward, instead of trying to get something out of the relationship.
- Remember to *maximize for happiness,* not for money or status.
- Think about what your *definition of success* really is. Is it externally driven or internally driven?
- Success unshared is failure. *Give back.* Share your wealth.
- *Values and ethics* always come first.

Their comments align wonderfully with what my experience has taught me contributes to lasting happiness and is reflective of a positive living legacy.

PURPOSE AND SPIRITUAL CAPITAL

Purpose and meaning are reflected as attributes contributing to happiness. Purpose is one of the three variables in my spiritual capital equation. For most of us, knowing how to answer the question "What is my purpose?" is not easy. As a matter of fact, it may take some time to be clear about this, and our purpose may shift at different times in our lives. But the *pursuit* of knowing our purpose is itself of great value. Unlike the pursuit of material abundance, which can only leave us, at a minimum, with short-lived happiness and, in worst-case scenarios, great despair, pursuing our purpose will provide us with passion, energy, and lasting happiness.

Harvard Business School professor Clayton M. Christensen is known to have his students answer three questions, two of which are these.[13]

- "How can I be sure that I will be successful and happy in my career?"
- "How can I be sure that my relationships with my spouse and my family will become an enduring source of happiness?"

In an article entitled "How Will You Measure Your Life?" that appeared in *Harvard Business Review* in July 2010, he states that he believes the pursuit of a profession is one way to achieve purpose, but without a purpose "life can become hollow."[14] In describing the significance of purpose in his own life, he also writes:

When I was a Rhodes Scholar, I was in a very demanding academic program, trying to cram an extra year's worth of work into my time at Oxford. I decided to spend an hour every night reading, thinking, and praying about why God

put me on this earth. That was a very challenging com-
mitment to keep, because every hour I spent doing that,
I wasn't studying applied econometrics. I was conflicted
about whether I could really afford to take that time away
from my studies, but I stuck with it--and ultimately fig-
ured out the purpose of my life.[15]

With just six months to live at age forty-eight, Randy Pausch, a professor of computer science at Carnegie Mellon, reflected on his life lessons learned and what he wanted to leave his three children, Dylan (then six years old), Logan (then three years old), and Chloe (then eighteen months old), and his wife, Jai. In his book *The Last Lecture* (Hyperion, 2008), Randy wrote about the memories he had of them, so they would know these as they grew up.

"I love all three of my kids completely and differently. And I want them to know that I love them for as long as they live." As a way to capture his legacy, he'd made videos, saved various letters, and wrote the book. In terms of what hopes he had for his children's lives, he writes:

A parent's job is to encourage kids to develop a joy for life
and a great urge to follow their own dreams. . . . So my
dreams for my kids are very exact: I want them to find their
own path to fulfillment. And given that I won't be there, I
want to make this clear: Kids, don't try to figure out what
I wanted you to become. I want you to become what you
want to become.[16]

Telling them to "find your own path to fulfillment" and "I want you to become what you want to become" is another way of sug-gesting to his children that they pursue the answer to the question

"What is my purpose?" This helps them to live their own legacies in life.

Being clear on our core values and our purpose, and multiplying these by our faith, can only lead us and others to achieve greater happiness. Faith, in particular, provides us with the "fuel" to maximize our values and purpose. As we have learned, having a purpose bigger than ourselves will contribute to lasting happiness and well-being. That larger purpose can be our family's well-being, eliminating a particular disease, and/or knowing our God. It is up to each of us to define our purpose and legacy for ourselves.

Frank Perdue, the well-known head of the Perdue family, which farms chickens, reflected his beliefs in his ethical will, written to help guide future generations of his family. This has been circulated on the Internet. Two of the ethical will's guidelines are:

- Remember that the way to be happy is to think of what you can do for others. The way to be miserable is to think about what people should be doing for you.
- Be a part of something bigger than your own self. That something can be family, pursuit of knowledge, the environment, or whatever you choose.[17]

Leveraging our spiritual GPS will navigate us toward lasting happiness and well-being. It will move us from success to significance. But we have to be intentional about pursuing it. Intention is critical to the matter. It's just as founding father Benjamin Franklin once said: "The Constitution only guarantees the American People the right to pursue happiness. You have to catch it yourself."[18]

It has been said that money can't buy happiness, but this is not true. It can. However it only can when we ensure that our financial capital serves our passions, signature strengths, and higher purpose, and by sharing it with others. This is the same recipe for optimizing our family wealth decisions and living a positive legacy.

I trust that after reading this chapter, you can now help me address Michelle, Himanshu, Nanda, and Darren's requests to help them and their children "be happy." More importantly, I trust that you now have a deeper understanding and skills to practice to contribute to your happiness and of those you love—to make the most of your legacy.

If you haven't yet formalized your estate plan or if you have the ability to adapt your existing estate plan, I encourage you to factor in the attributes of happiness. Think of this as part of your legacy planning. For example, do not only set up your trusts to focus on what I refer to as external milestones, such as college graduation, reaching a certain age, and securing a full-time job; or preventing what you do not want to happen in the lives of beneficiaries, such as substance abuse, laziness, and so forth. Instead, incentivize the attributes that will contribute to happiness: identifying and pursuing dreams, sharing our capitals with others, and so forth. Similarly, if you decide to give to charities and others outside your family, ensure that your gifts and donations are governed first and foremost by your spiritual capital and the recipients' happiness. Also select trustees and guardians who will mentor your children to live happy lives, not just help ensure they "don't turn out wrong."

As importantly, if you fully leverage your spiritual capital and the attributes that lead to lasting happiness in your parenting, it will significantly increase the odds that you will contribute to a well-prepared next generation, which is discussed further in Chapter 5. It has been said that money is like fire: It can warm our feet or it can burn our socks off. I trust that you are now better equipped to ensure that your financial capital will warm your socks and the socks of those you love.

Below is a list that reflects the happiness attributes mentioned earlier in the chapter. Before you move on to the next chapter, take a few moments to rate yourself for each. In whichever areas you rate lower, begin to practice these attributes each day and then watch your happiness grow.

On a scale of 1–5, where 1 means never, 2 means rarely, 3 means sometimes, 4 means often, and 5 means always, to what extent are you utilizing the following attributes. Circle your answers.

GIVING BACK/SHARING WITH OTHERS

1   2   3   4   5

FINDING PURPOSE AND MEANING

1   2   3   4   5

CHERISHING RELATIONSHIPS

1   2   3   4   5

BEING GRATEFUL

1   2   3   4   5

PRACTICING FORGIVENESS TOWARD SELF AND OTHERS

1   2   3   4   5

BEING PLAYFUL

1   2   3   4   5

BEING OPEN

1   2   3   4   5

BEING TRUE TO YOURSELF

1   2   3   4   5

ACHIEVING WORTHWHILE GOALS

1   2   3   4   5

HAVING FAITH

1   2   3   4   5

CHAPTER FOUR
TRANSFERRING YOUR WEALTH

"Wealth does not pass three generations."
—Chinese proverb

was talking to Clare, the granddaughter of a successful wealth creator. Clare was in her thirties and married, with two children. She shared with me that although she and her parents and siblings were fortunate to have lived a privileged lifestyle consisting of luxury travel, beautiful homes, private schools, and other material possessions, she didn't feel like the wealth was hers. And to date, it literally wasn't. Very little of the prior two generations' wealth had been transferred to Clare and her siblings, yet she had always lived her life as if she was personally wealthy.

When I asked Clare if she knew what her parents' or grandparents' net worth was, she said, "I really don't know." I asked her if she was anticipating inheriting any of their wealth one day, and again she replied, "I really don't know." She went on to say, "Although my grandparents created the wealth, people don't appreciate how hard it has been for my parents to maintain it."

My next question to Clare was, "What is the mission you and your siblings have for the family's wealth should it transfer to you one day and you become wealth holders?" I was attempting to discover if her family had addressed its financial legacy. Once again, Clare replied, "I really don't know."

Clare and her family are not alone. Most affluent families don't ever talk about their wealth, even among themselves; nor do most wealth holders properly prepare their children and grandchildren for their eventual inheritance. This lack of communication and preparation has a direct impact on the legacy of multiple generations at the same time. And the lack of planning inhibits optimizing this very important family wealth decision: How do we transfer wealth to our descendants and heirs? In the majority of cases, the assets are prepared for the family, but the family is rarely prepared properly for the assets.

"Shirtsleeves to shirtsleeves in three generations" is the American equivalent of the Chinese proverb "Wealth does not pass three generations." The same phenomenon is found throughout the world, where it is referenced by different phrases. In England, they say, "Clogs to clogs in three generations." In Italy it is, "From the stables to the stars to the stables in three generations."[1] It is well known in countries around the world that someone in the first gener-

In the majority of cases, the assets are prepared for the family, but the family is rarely prepared properly for the assets.

ation of an affluent family works really hard to create wealth. The second generation reaps the benefits of the wealth, and the third generation is likely to squander it.

Another way of describing this common, though not inevitable phenomenon, is to say that the first generation creates, the second preserves, and the third consumes.

Interestingly enough, the failure to transfer money to, and beyond, the third generation does not usually result from the original wealth owners' failure to put a solid financial and estate plan in place, as most people would assume. Nor does the failure usually stem from the fact that the wealth is dissipated by being passed into the hands of a larger group of people. The primary reasons that family wealth dissipates in a few generations are a breakdown in communication and trust within the family, and the lack of readiness of the heirs to receive the wealth.[2] They have not adequately addressed matters relevant to their legacy.

As I talked to Clare, it became obvious that her family was living out the reality of the proverbs. There was little communication in her family about their wealth, and she and her siblings had received no intentional preparation. During a series of conversations that ensued between us, I also learned that there was tension and a lack of trust between various family members. It soon was evident to me that this family would lose its wealth unless the members of the different generations changed what they were doing.

To Clare's credit, she had decided that she would be proactive by going to her parents and opening up a conversation about their wealth and her probable inheritance of some of it, as well as by trying to be a catalyst for improving family relationships across the board.

LEVERAGING YOUR SPIRITUAL CAPITAL

Often, it is the work of the elder generations to align family estate planning with spiritual capital. Sometimes it is the work of members of the younger generation, leveraging their spiritual capital in order to optimize this important family wealth decision and family legacy. The latter was such a case for Clare and her family.

The decision to transfer wealth to children and grandchildren is a multidimensional and sophisticated decision. All children are not cut from the same cloth even when they come from the same biological family. Where they are in their life cycles will impact their maturity levels and also their perspectives on the world. Baby Boomers, Gen Xers, and Millennials often have different perspectives, for example. Other factors, such as fluctuating asset levels, individual life choices, addictions and other psychological problems, and the unknowns of life (marriage, birth, sudden death, special needs, job loss, market forces, tax law changes, and the geopolitical climate) can have an impact on your important family decisions, and especially on your wealth-transferring decisions.

Many books, techniques, and technically competent professionals are available to help families break the shirtsleeves-to-shirtsleeves phenomenon. Even so, the statistics are still dismal. The reality is that most wealth, like most family businesses, does not last beyond the second generation. The majority does not even survive to reach the third. Too many people are still navigating their major decisions using the equivalent of "paper maps." As for other types of decisions that are discussed in this book, you will benefit greatly if you upgrade your decision-making processes related to wealth transfer by leveraging your spiritual capital, that hidden key in your life that is most secure, reliable, and taps into the "heavens."

This chapter assumes you intend to transfer wealth to the

next generation; and also that you have decided to structure a plan to transfer your wealth by focusing on the *how.* Remember that your *whats, whys,* and *hows* must come together for an intended living and lasting legacy to be effective. Many wealth creators and holders decide to share their wealth both during their lives and upon their deaths with people outside their immediate families: people such as close friends, significant others, and extended family, for example. Those decisions will be covered here. Giving to other entities and organizations, however, will be addressed in Chapter 6.

Sharing wealth with descendants and heirs is a consideration for almost every successful individual, including those that do not have children and those who are life partners and yet are not married in the traditional sense. The overall process I advocate can be applied wonderfully to all scenarios. Your spiritual capital is transcendent in function and needs to be applied uniquely to each situation, child, and family structure—for example, a blended family.

Finally, in this chapter we will cover the work you should preferably complete prior to creating an estate plan. If you have a plan in place already, after completing the work described here, check to ensure that your estate plan is in alignment with the process provided, and if it is not, update it if at all possible. That being said, in no way should the fact that you've done the work presented below negate the absolute necessity to integrate this work with the counsel of the most competent and trusted professional advisors you know. Remember, making decisions with the perspective of spiritual capital is not about negating traditional tools; it's about integrating them with the new technology of your spiritual GPS.

The process you are about to learn has five steps.

STEP 1: ESTABLISH YOUR VALUES, PURPOSE, AND FAITH

It was late afternoon on a beautiful spring day. I was waiting in the elegantly designed conference room of my new client's company. I'd had a previous phone conversation with the patriarch in this particular family, but had not yet met him or his wife face to face. During the phone conversation with this man, who was the wealth creator in his family, he let me know that he and his wife wanted some guidance, as they were beginning their legacy planning. He had already accumulated wealth and was expecting an additional increase in the near future.

As I gazed out of large conference room windows overlooking a beautiful landscape, I heard the conference room door open. I turned and found myself facing a man and woman in their mid-forties. "Great to meet you, Mr. and Mrs. Paulson," I said.

They replied, "Great to meet you as well, and please, call us Phil and Marla."

After some initial welcoming and introductory conversation, I said, "Today we will focus on your responses and thoughts to the questions about purpose and faith sent to you in preparation of this meeting." Those questions, which were covered earlier in the book, included things like: "What do you believe is the purpose of your wealth?" and "Do you have a faith or spiritual perspective that influences your financial and estate planning decisions?" I continued, "In addition, today we will complete a values exercise together. The compilation of these two efforts will prepare you well to sit with your other trusted advisors and begin drafting your estate plan."

Although the process used that day with Phil and Marla varies in duration depending on my clients' situation and unique needs, it typically starts with having the client or clients reflect upon, and respond to a set of non-technical questions, such as the ones that follow, to determine the kind of imprint they wish to make on their family and the world with their time, talent, and treasures. In this case, we reviewed the answers together.

- What is your intended legacy?
- What is the multigenerational vision of your wealth?
- What concerns might you have about your wealth?
- What percentage of your wealth are you considering transferring to the ones you love versus spending, versus donating to charities?
- If you have a blended family consisting of children from prior relationships, are you intending to share your wealth equally across all the children?

There are various ways to help individuals, couples, and families identify their core values, and one of the ways I do this is by using a values card-sorting exercise based on the five capitals. (Values cards can be purchased by going to: LegacyCapitals.com/store.) The cards reflect values statements, such as the ones in the box below.

VALUES

- A global mindset
- A minimum level of financial literacy
- Adventure
- Beauty
- Being adaptive
- Being part of a faith-based community
- Broad-mindedness

- Compassion
- Competence
- Creativity
- Excitement
- Family coherence
- Family travel
- Financial independence
- Financial security
- Friendship

- Generosity
- Good reputation
- Having a strong work ethic
- Health
- Honesty
- Including children in my acts of philanthropy
- Independence
- Intelligence
- Leading a spiritual life
- Learning
- Living a life of moderation
- Living a purposeful life
- Loyalty
- Peace/harmony
- Personal safety/security
- Pleasure
- Power
- Preparing next-generation leaders
- Professional achievement
- Purpose
- Recognition
- Respecting others
- Self-discipline
- Sharing/donating time and talents
- Social justice
- Tradition
- Wisdom

After handing Phil and Marla a set of cards, I said, "Let's begin. Individually, choose your top ten values from the cards." After giving them enough time to identify and prioritize their values, I then asked them to share their prioritized values out loud. Marla volunteered to go first. She had picked cards that read: "Using our resources to making a positive impact," "work ethic," "spending quality time as a family," and others.

Before Phil began to read his choices, he said, "I agree with everything Marla shared." He then read his own selections, which were: "faith," "professional achievement," "teaching stewardship to our children," and others.

From the card exercise and from their responses to the questions sent to Phil and Marla before our meeting, it was clear that they were aligned in their values. Furthermore, both wanted to ensure that their financial capital always served their values, intended legacy, and provided opportunities for individual and family growth, a mutually held purpose. They also wanted to make sure that each of their four children developed a strong work ethic, as a part of the legacy of their parenting. Phil remarked, "I don't want our wealth to take off their 'edge.'"

In addition to giving to their children, the couple knew they wanted to donate money to several organizations they were involved with that reflected their values and intended legacy. Phil and Marla shared a faith that fostered the value known as "stewardship." "Although we have worked real hard to earn what we have, we know it is still God's, and we are responsible for being the best stewards of it," Marla said.

It is worth noting that Phil and Marla had each brought two children into their marriage from prior relationships, and had decided that whatever amount of wealth they decided to transfer to their children would be shared equally. The one place that Phil and Marla did not originally see eye-to-eye was regarding an initial thought of Phil's that they would create one trust that all four children would share. Marla had concern that given the very different personalities of the children, it would be better to have a separate trust for each child.

Her point was a valid one. In my experience, when there exists a shared family resource—whether it is a trust, a company, a home, or a boat—a level of skill and governance is required for siblings to negotiate its usage and sometimes its sale, especially after the parents are deceased.

So you may be wondering, "How did this work connect to their actual estate planning?" Good question. Here's how. Remember some of their priorities and values: stewardship, work ethic, family, giving back, and so forth. Phil and Marla decided that they would create a family foundation to formally give back, a separate trust for each of the children, and a shared trust so that all four still had a reason to work and be together. The value of stewardship led them to create dynasty trusts for each of the children so that, if possible, the *corpus* (the technical term referring to the property or assets that are transferred to a trust) would be available for future generations.

Other than for special needs or specific opportunities, the children would not inherit or have access to the wealth until Phil and Marla passed away. They believed that if their children received a lot of wealth too soon (a relative definition for each individual and family) it could take away their work ethic, or as Phil said, "Their edge." When we were done with our work together, Phil and Marla's priorities, wishes, and intentions were then taken to their other trusted advisors (in this case, an attorney and a private banker) to be integrated with their absolutely necessary and wise guidance regarding tax, asset protection, and wealth preservation.

The Paulsons' situation and goals may not reflect your situation or your goals, however the process of articulating and codifying your *values,* being clear on the *purpose* of your life and wealth, and leveraging your *faith* or spiritual beliefs (whatever they may be) is fundamental and vital as you work through how you plan to transfer your wealth to future generations of your family (or to any others you love and care about).

If you are thinking, "I can see the importance of values and maybe even purpose, but faith or spirituality?" or "I don't have a faith like the Paulsons'" or "I believe spiritual matters are for the "religious," I understand. Hang in there with me a little longer and more will become clear.

TAKING TIME TO ALIGN WITH YOUR FAITH

One might ask, "Why should I reach out to God (or the Divine) regarding financial matters?" Another might ask, "Why should one not reach out to God (or the Divine)?" to seek further wisdom when making big decisions that have an impact on others and one's living legacy?"

The faith variable in your spiritual capital equation is not about being religious or adopting someone else's faith. Each person's faith is personal, even if that faith involves there being no Divinity. However, if you do not tap fully into some form of higher wisdom you may be missing out on important and timeless guidance. It appears only prudent to do so.

To put this another way, using the urban nomenclature of our day: Are you "dialed in"? When you turn on the radio in your car is the radio silent, or is there a lot of static drowning out the music? When you adjust the dial just right, the music on the radio station comes in clear, allowing you to sit back and enjoy both it and the ride. Similarly, when you dial in to your higher wisdom, do you get static, silence, or insights? (Pardon the additional radio metaphor, but it is analogous to having clarity about our values, purpose, and faith and being intentional in how we use them.)

There are many variables and moving parts to factor into your important family wealth decisions, not the least of which are your own internal beliefs and past experiences with wealth. It could only be helpful, therefore, if you set aside time to reflect on, meditate, or pray about the important decisions you are about to make that can affect the overall well-being of others. Maybe wrapping your mind around the intangibles of life, such as how to tap into your spiritual dimension while you're also in the process of making important tangible decisions about your financial capital isn't easy. Nonetheless, this doesn't make it any less valuable to do so.

As discussed throughout this book, you may have experienced a continuum of spiritual, or intangible, experiences that are hard to measure and fully explain. These experiences have rung true to you. Listening to Beethoven's Ninth Symphony, watching *Les Miserables*, holding your baby shortly after birth, seeing the smile on the face of another because of the investment you made in his or her life, communing with nature, walking through the Louvre Museum, sitting on the beach at sunrise, meditating, and praying to God are just a short list of the many ways one may experiences the Divine. Usually during such moments we gain perspective, step out of our present circumstances, and become clearer about what matters most to us.

I was having a coffee with one of my clients, the CEO of a rapidly growing company. He jokingly told me that those who report directly to him like to call him right after he finishes one of his yoga classes because they know, "It is then that I have the most lucid and gracious mindset, and they are more likely to get what they ask for." Similarly, it is important for you to find a spiritual practice for yourself that allows you to stack the cards in your favor when making the important family wealth decisions in your life. My client's lucidity and graciousness are elements of his legacy that routinely impact the lives of his employees, and through them the customers and vendors they serve, and their families. His human capital was directly benefitted by his investment into his spiritual capital.

Set aside time on an ongoing basis and, especially before you make any important decisions like transferring wealth to others, create moments to align inwardly with God or the Divine. In your own way, be still and listen. Ask: "Is there any other perspective I need on this matter?" When I practice this myself, my path is made clearer and my hunches are confirmed. I also find that by adjusting my vision to a broader perspective new possibilities emerge.

STEP 2: INVENTORY YOUR BELIEFS AND PAST EXPERIENCES

The first step in every important family wealth decision process is programming your spiritual capital. However, there are other strategic steps to take in your wealth transfer planning. One of these important next steps is to assess your own internal beliefs, or mental scripts, about money, money messages you've received, and your past experiences with wealth. These are a form of intellectual capital that can be viewed as a *mental legacy*.

As you might imagine, there is a continuum of beliefs and messages any one person can hold. My own clients have shared beliefs with me that range from "Money only causes problems" to "You can never have too much."

Here are a handful of other common ones. See if any seem familiar to you.

- "You can't trust people when it comes to money."
- "If I give money to others, then they will love and care for me."
- "Even though you live in our home, it is not your money."
- "Others will only want you for your money."
- "It is not our wealth, it is God's."

From time to time, I like to reference the famous comment made by Socrates at the end of his trial, "The unexamined life is not worth living,"[3] and put my twist on it. It's my contention that your unexamined beliefs about money and your experiences with money will manifest somewhere in your estate planning. Therefore, it is important to acknowledge them, and then to consciously determine if they should be perpetuated. Are your beliefs and values the best fit for those who will inherit from you and share in your wealth? Is this a legacy you intend to share?

There is a scene in the documentary *Born Rich* by Jamie

Johnson, in which Jamie Johnson (one of the third-generation inheritors of the Johnson & Johnson fortune) is talking to his father (also an inheritor, rather than an original creator) in front of a fireplace. In short, the dialogue reflects an awkward, but honest discussion between a father and son reflecting two different perspectives on the family wealth. Each man had lived a different legacy along with his inheritance. The father reflects that he hasn't ever been quite comfortable with the wealth, whereas the son is clearly trying to ensure that he is psychologically happy and comfortable with the wealth.[4]

One of the most common money messages that is given to the next generation of wealth inheritors is, "This is not your money; this is our money." Because I commonly work with multiple generations of the same family, I usually hear several sides of the same conversation. Parents generally communicate this message because they do not want their children to develop a mindset of entitlement. From the parents' view, they want to establish a work ethic in their children—this is the legacy they intend to pass on. From the children's perspective, those who hear this message often interpret it to mean that they are privileged and very fortunate, but it also makes them nervous about what to expect and how to prepare. Are they good enough and doing the right things?

The lines between money and love are often blurred.

The other common message that children receive is actually not a verbal message. Instead, the family wealth is not talked about—in a manner reminiscent of Clare's family. As a result, there is no opportunity for either the parent or the inheritor to properly prepare. Then, when the money is eventually transferred, the recipient has a "sudden money" experience that is usually a bit jolting, to say the least.

As you plan for the eventual transfer of your wealth, set time aside to answer the following questions:

- What are your core money beliefs?
- What messages about wealth were passed on to you?
- What experiences of wealth have been awkward or stressful for you?
- What experiences of wealth have been entirely positive experiences?

It is important for you to have your responses to these questions in your pocket before you begin to plan to transfer your wealth to your children or other heirs, otherwise you might leave them an unintended legacy of harmful beliefs.

STEP 3: DETERMINE WHAT YOU WANT TO TRANSFER

Another important step is to ask the qualitative question, "*What* do you want to transfer or enable in your beneficiaries' lives?" rather than starting with the all too often quantitative question of, "How much should I transfer?" Putting it another way, I often ask my clients, "What guardrails or support structures do you want to put in your children's lives?"

More questions, among others that typically come up at this step, are:

- Do you want to ensure that their college education is paid for?
- Do you want to make sure the ones you love and care about always have health care?
- Will you provide an entrepreneur fund to enable your children to start companies when they're ready?
- Will you match your children's personal donations to charities?
- Will you give extra to your adult son and his wife because they have a special needs child?

After answering these questions and others that occur to you, you can back into determining the number you would need to transfer in order to enable your particular and specific whats to happen. Let me give you an example of this step in practice.

It was my first meeting with Mr. and Mrs. Stein. When I asked how I could help, they said, "We decided that we want to give some of our wealth to our children in the near future and not wait until we pass away." Mr. and Mrs. Stein had three children ranging in age from twenty-one to thirty-two. They went on to say that they were not intending to give each child the same amount, and instead were thinking of starting by giving one million dollars to their oldest child, though they were not sure what to give the other two. I asked them to tell me more about each of their children and give some details about their relationships with them as individuals.

I learned that the oldest child, a daughter, was going through a divorce and had a young child. They recognized her need for help with her finances. They also referred to her as the "responsible one." They felt the others were less responsible. "Our second child has still not found himself, and our third sometimes acts spoiled," said Mr. Stein. "This is why we want to give our oldest a million and we aren't sure what amount to give to the others." Mrs. Stein added, "We are very close to our oldest daughter and close with our youngest, but there is some distance and tension between us and our middle child."

I went on to work closely with the Steins for the next couple of months, taking them through the same process of inventorying their values and beliefs as with the Paulsons, and which you will have done if you are following my advice in this book. When that work was complete, I asked them not to think about how much they wanted to transfer, and instead to start with what they were trying to accomplish by transferring their wealth. What were the needs of each child, and *what* was most important to them to give him or her?

At the end of the process, they had decided on the following:

1. They would, in fact, transfer some of their wealth to their children while they were alive so they could witness and enjoy the benefits of the money in their children's lives. However, they decided to wait another year before making this happen so that they would have more time to prepare their children for the money they would receive.

2. They would *not* give an equal amount initially, considering the unique situations and maturity levels of each child. In fact, they decided to give more than one million to each of the three children, but would place different terms on how and when each child would have access to the corpus and income it produced.

3. They would set up a family foundation to begin formally giving some of their wealth away, and they would invite all of their children to be involved in their charitable giving.

4. The preceding three decisions would be taken to attorneys and financial advisers to work out on paper in the most strategically tax efficient and asset protective manner possible.

Another example of determining what to transfer (versus how much) reminds me of a conversation I had with a matriarch named Sarah, who was working on her estate plan. We were sitting in Sarah's kitchen with her financial advisor, talking about her family and goals for her planning. Among others, one of Sarah's goals was to transfer some amount of wealth to her sons' wives separately from the money she planned to transfer to her sons. She told me the reason for this was because it was what her mother-in-law had done for her. This was a legacy she wanted to continue passing on to the next generation of women in the family.

Sarah shared that her mother-in-law had transferred to all her daughter-in-laws some amount of wealth with the message, "I believe women should have wealth of their own." This message had left such a positive and indelible impression on her that she wanted to pay it forward.

You can see from the examples above that if my clients had started with the quantitative "How much?" question, they were unlikely to arrive at what they really wanted to accomplish in the lives of others. And likely their decisions would have not been fully aligned with their spiritual capital.

Another reason it is important to be clear first on what you are intending to transfer is because it can help you with the "fair versus equal" question that may emerge, unless you decide to transfer your assets equally across the board with all children, grandchildren, and others you love and care about. All too often wealth creators and wealth holders get caught up in being perceived as unfair to one family member or another.

To help my clients mitigate this possibility, I ask them to think about their whats across two dimensions: horizontal and vertical. The horizontal dimension refers to what they will pass on equally to all potential inheritors: values; opportunities; health care costs, if needed; down payments on a first home; tuition for college; and so forth.

The vertical dimension takes into account the unique needs of the individuals.

Using the two-dimensional approach, wealth holders can think about the ways their inheritors are able to share equally in their wealth, and the other ways that the only fair course of action is to customize their approach given the situation of a specific inheritor. For example, a special needs child.

STEP 4: TRANSFER OR GIFT?

Determining if you are *transferring* your wealth or *gifting* your wealth to your children (and other heirs) is another important step in your planning. I am not talking about the technical definition of gifting assets to another, which has a tax benefit. Instead, I am referring to the qualitative nature of your decision: the spirit of the decision and not the letter of the law.

At the heart of this matter is the issue of control: What level of control do you want to retain over the assets directly, as a trustee, and/or indirectly through the terms you establish for your heirs' access to the assets? These are personal decisions to be determined by you, the wealth transmitter, in consideration of your thoughts about the wealth receiver (a child, an extended family member, a lover, or even a friend). Furthermore, these are not either-or decisions.

For illustrative purposes, think of gifting assets to others, in the non-technical sense, as giving money and other assets with no strings attached to it. In this way, it is truly like a birthday gift to someone you love.

By contrast, transferring assets to another person connotes that the transfer has some, if not many, strings attached to it—as you might do when transferring assets to young children.

I remember talking to a matriarch who clearly stated to me, "If I haven't raised my children right by now (they were already in their thirties and forties) then it is my fault, so once they receive the assets, they are theirs. I want nothing to do with the assets after that."

On the other side of the control spectrum, I remember sitting in one of the most opulent homes in the United States with the matriarch and patriarch of another family, listening to them rattle off all the conditions that had to be met if their children were going to inherit any more of their wealth. In this case, the "children" were adults with their own families, and living, at least by most people's standards, fairly responsible lives.

This leads me to the next important point, which is that all too often the decision of whether to gift or to transfer is made by focusing exclusively on the wealth transmitter's perspective. I understand this default position, given the fact that the transmitter created the wealth and/or is presently the wealth holder. However, using your own point of view as the starting and ending point in making the decision may not always be the best approach.

I am not suggesting you sit down with the eventual receivers of your wealth and say, "Hey, how much and when would you like to receive our wealth?" Instead, consider, to the best of your ability to do so, the potential impact of the transfer or gift on the recipients. Will the wealth enhance their lives, contribute to their overall well-being, and lead them to fulfill their dreams rather than yours? Or might it unintentionally hinder or dampen their lives? A key to optimizing wealth decisions is to anticipate these hidden psychological and emotional legacies that are being passed on with the financial capital.

As you may know, there are stages in the life cycle of a butterfly that are reflected in its transformation from a caterpillar to a butterfly. *The transition stage* is the time when the caterpillar, now called a pupa, is protected inside of a cocoon made of silk. Although it is hard to see from the outside, big changes are happening inside. Special cells that were present in the caterpillar are now growing rapidly. These will become the legs, wings, eyes, and other parts of the adult butterfly.

This internal struggle before breaking out of the cocoon as a beautiful butterfly is vital to its survival. It is the very struggle that produces its growth and transformation. If you felt the desire to help a struggling pupa change faster or easier, and so decided to chip away at its silk cocoon, you would actually prevent the pupa from becoming a butterfly, and would end its life.

Similarly, it is typically a parent's instinct (and true for most human beings) to want to take care of, and provide for their children and others. And when you have a lot of financial resources you can do just this. However, as you think about how much you will give your children and the timing of your giving, you must consider what stage of their life cycle they are in, so that you don't unintentionally prevent them from learning to fly.

I commonly ask my clients, "Do you love your children enough *not* to give them everything you can?" By this I mean, do you wish to leave them a legacy of responsibility, resilience, and opportunities for learning and self-mastery?

Having said all this, if you have open, two-way communication and high levels of trust with the children you are intending to transfer wealth to, and they are responsible and productive people, then it may be appropriate to consult with them about your decision. Consulting with them still does not equate to saying, "Hey, how much and when would you like to receive our wealth?" However, it does suggest that gathering their thoughts, feelings, and ideas about a particular scenario could be helpful input for you before you make your ultimate decision.

I can think of the following two scenarios where this type of dialogue could be very helpful. The first scenario is when your family has a family business and not all family members work in it. The family has decided to sell the business, a decision that will result in the creation of a lot of liquid wealth. Should all family members share equally in the sale? Is it fair to ask the family members who helped build it with their blood, sweat, and tears to share equally with other family members who have chosen to do otherwise?

Having an open, honest dialogue with the entire family to brainstorm ideas on how to find your balance between fair and equal can be beneficial in such scenarios. Sometimes just the step of asking for other family members' opinions can go a long way toward creating harmony in the family and the satisfaction of being heard and valued. I once worked with a very close, trusting and high-functioning family with a family business. They decided that all family members would share equally in the sale of their company even though not all family members had worked in the business. They understood the emotional legacy of being connected to the business was equally as real as the financial legacy; that the two legacies were inextricably linked.

The other scenario that comes to mind is when grandparents want to share their wealth with their grandchildren, but each of their children does not have the same amount of, or any, offspring. This dynamic is reflected in a choice between *per stirpes* and *per capita* options. Per stirpes, in this scenario, is when you decide to transfer wealth equally through each adult child (the parents of the grandchildren). Per capita is when you decide to divide the amount you are giving based on the total number of grandchildren. Needing to make this choice might come up, for example, in a situation where education is highly valued by grandparents who want to fund their grandchildren's education, yet not all of their adult children are married or have the same amount or any children. How can the grandparents be fair in this situation?

Assuming the family variables mentioned above, asking the adult children how they (the grandparents) can go about this fairly would not only create a legacy of good will, but could also generate real creative options. One family I worked with decided to have the grandparents give an equal amount of wealth to each child, while saying, "We would like you to use this gift toward the education of your children or grandchildren one day, but if this doesn't fit your situation, then please use it however you see fit."

STEP 5: TRANSFER YOUR WEALTH WHILE YOU'RE ALIVE, OR AFTER DEATH?

A remaining next step in your wealth transfer planning process is to decide if you want to transfer or gift some or all of your assets while you are alive and/or after you have passed away.

There are a number of benefits to transferring some of your assets while you are alive. The first benefit is the ability to see how the inheritor receives and responds to the inheritance. Are they good stewards? Do they invest in their passions and life goals? Does it cause them to trip up? This provides them with the opportunity to learn and grow, and you can be part of this wonderful process. There is a case to be made that it is better to fail fast when they are younger when there is less on the line (for example, significantly smaller amount of assets).

Giving while you are alive can also help you determine how you might plan to transfer, gift, or donate the rest of your assets to a particular heir, or not, at some other point, or points, in time. I remember sitting in a family meeting with the parents and their five adult children, who were in their twenties and thirties. The dad said to his children, "Mom and I believe we have already given you all that we should financially, the rest will be determined by how much we decide to give away and how you continue to live your lives." He meant he wanted to see the kinds of choices they made before he extended further generosity.

The other benefit is the joy, happiness, and internal rewards you can experience as a result of seeing the fruits of your labor benefit others. Legacy is a two-way street: By benefitting someone else, you can gain immense satisfaction. For example, remember the Stein's oldest daughter who had a young child and was going through a divorce? She didn't have much money and soon was going to be a single mom. Imagine the stress that would leave her heart and mind by having her parents pay off her mortgage.

Or what if you had a close friend or an extended family member who worked hard, but also had to face various challenges in his life? Imagine the look on his face if you sent him and his family on a paid vacation to a place of their dreams.

There are abundant opportunities to share your resources and five capitals with others that will be addressed later in the book.

UPDATING YOUR LIVING LEGACY

Intentionally following the five steps I've just laid out, starting with your values, purpose, and faith will surely help you to create an estate plan and, in general, a life plan that will be closely aligned with your values, beliefs, and intentions, and also with that which is best for the people with whom you plan to share your wealth.

In most cases, an estate plan needs to be updated periodically as financial circumstances change, spouses and grandchildren are added to the family, and/or you and your significant other grow and have shifts in your perspective.

My wife and I established our estate plan a number of years back and recently were scheduled to have our children join us on a trip to a family reunion across the country. This wouldn't be the first time we were all on a plane together, but it was going to be the first time that my parents, my siblings, and their families would be on the same plane with us. It literally caused my wife and me to update our estate plan should the worst-case scenario happen. Fortunately tragedy didn't occur, but we did update our estate plan to reflect what would happen to our assets if so many of our closest family members were no longer around. It was a very reflective and provocative exercise to work through. In fact, it took our discussion of our values, purpose, and faith to a whole new level.

I trust this chapter has caused you to think about the role

of your spiritual capital in successful wealth transfer. The first step of grounding yourself by prioritizing your values not only will provide you with your secure foundation for decision making, it will also help you navigate the next four steps. What you value, the purpose of your wealth, and the investment into your spiritual life will absolutely help you evaluate your beliefs about wealth, decide what you want to pass on, determine whether you are transferring or gifting your wealth, and if you plan to transfer your wealth in your lifetime or after you passed away—or some combination of both.

The next chapter will focus on how to prepare the next generation for the wealth transfer.

SUMMARY
A FIVE-STEP, NON-TECHNICAL PROCESS FOR TRANSFERRING YOUR WEALTH

Step 1: Establish your values, purpose, and faith (the three variables of your spiritual capital).

Step 2: Inventory your beliefs about wealth and your experiences with wealth.

Step 3: Determine what you want to transfer versus how much.

Step 4: Decide: Are you transferring and/or gifting your wealth?

Step 5: Decide: Will you transfer during your lifetime and/or upon your death?

CHAPTER FIVE

NEXT-GENERATION PREPARATION

"Life is no brief candle to me. It is a sort of splendid torch which I have got a hold of for the moment, and I want to make it burn as brightly as possible before handing it on to future generations."
—George Bernard Shaw

"We need to teach the next generation of children from day one that they are responsible for their lives. Mankind's greatest gift, also its greatest curse, is that we have free choice. We can make our choices built from love or from fear."
—Elisabeth Kübler-Ross

Institutional clients of mine recently asked me to attend their one-day "next generation" conference in order to provide them feedback and advise how they could perhaps make the conference "even better" in the future. About seventy-five advisors of different kinds, from estate attorneys to wealth managers, all who serve affluent families, attended. The primary objective of the event was to help these professionals connect with, and successfully prepare the next generation of wealth holders to manage their inheritances.

Arriving a few minutes early, I grabbed a healthy snack being offered outside the ballroom in the four-star hotel at which the conference was held. Then I took my seat and waited with great anticipation for the program to start. The room filled up quickly and there was a buzz in the air.

The first presenter began right on time. She set the stage by talking about the next-generation opportunity for wealth advisors of serving clients whose trillions of dollars are being transferred from one generation to the next, and detailing topics relevant to affluent families, such as financial education. She made reference to family values. Each subsequent speaker built upon her opening comments and talked about the different ways they and their peers could educate their clients' children and grandchildren. For example, they could offer seminars on topics such as the difference between equities and fixed income, asset allocation, credit scores, budgeting, taxes, retirement planning, insurance, the basics of trusts, and the power of compound interest. One speaker, a wealth manager, shared some examples of how he worked one-on-one with the children of his clients to set up investment accounts. He spoke at length about Roth IRAs.

As I sat there that day, listening to the roster of speakers, I heard the same overall assumptions being repeated that I had previously read and heard about in other forums. The two core assumptions—with which I disagree—were, the primary importance of financial education in the lives of members of the next generation, and that all "next-gen" inheritors of wealth share the same needs and objectives. This is a one-dimensional way to understand and approach next-generation preparation. At the end of the day, I gave my client's conference an A in terms of design, speaker effectiveness, use of technology, and focused message. But it got a C in terms of accurately addressing the planning needs of those who will soon inherit wealth. After the conference I met my clients and we discussed ways to broaden the topics regarding next-generation preparation in future conferences.

Planning, at its best, should be a process of integration. Although financial education is an important aspect of the preparation of the next generation, it tends to overshadow other variables of planning that we have seen. In fact, these variables can be more relevant to whether or not members of the next generation live flourishing lives.

There are three primary reasons for the over-weighting of financial education in legacy planning. The first is that it's reflexive. Of course wealth must be managed appropriately to be maintained. But most of the time the wealth is actually managed by professionals outside of the family. The second reason is that other variables that matter are harder to count. Financial capital is more tangible than other capitals in the FISHS rubric. Intellectual capital, social capital, human capital, and spiritual capital are "softer," so planning for success in these areas can seem like a fuzzier topic to everyone involved in making big family decisions, especially those pertaining to their money and other assets.

The third reason is that members of the wealth industry naturally lead from their strengths and prefer to operate in their comfort zone. Similarly, when psychologists participate in next-generation preparation they typically overemphasize issues pertaining to the psychology of wealth, such as how family members feel about their wealth, or the internal relationship they have with their financial capital.

The intention of this chapter is to show you why next-generation preparation approached as a multidimensional and multi-generational process is most effective. How to prepare the next generation is one of the most important family wealth decisions that need to be optimized because of their potential impact on legacy across generations.

DEFINING THE NEXT GENERATION

Do all members of the next generation look the same, think the same, and have the same needs? Of course not. The next generation is diverse. It includes forty-somethings with their own children, college-aged sons and daughters, and five-year-olds who are just starting kindergarten. People of different ages are raised in different sociopolitical contexts that influence their perspectives on everything—and particularly views on money. If you were to do an Internet search on Traditionalists, Baby Boomers, Gen Xers, Millennials (aka Gen Yers), or Plurals (aka Gen Zers), you would find uniquely generational characteristics. Age is a dimension that impacts planning on many levels.

Should we talk about members of the next generation solely in terms of chronology? What about in terms of their relationship to the generation that creates significant wealth? Sons or daughters raised in a family where significant wealth was created when they were in their twenties would have a different perspective than children who were two. The former may have a conscious experience of becoming immersed in the context of significant wealth. The latter may take the same context for granted. I have seen this phenomenon reflected in blended families, for example, who bring children from different wealth backgrounds and of different ages.

When considering chronology commencing with the wealth-creating generation, a young adult, for example, raised four generations after significant wealth creation is likely to have a different perspective on inheritance than someone who is just one generation descended from a wealth creator.

Determining what we mean when we refer to members of the next generation reminds me of the classic Bud Abbott and Lou Costello skit "Who's on First?" It's a very funny play on words that illustrates the pitfalls of communication. Depending on your age, you may need to do a quick search online to watch the short video clip of their performance for the first time.

To avoid undergoing our own version of this skit, let's agree to focus on the relationship between two successive generations. The transmitters of wealth—aka, the parents or grantors —are the present-generation wealth holders. This is true whether they created the wealth themselves or have inherited it from members of a prior generation. The receivers of the wealth or future inheritors—aka, the children or beneficiaries—are the next generation.

I chose two quotes at the beginning of this chapter to represent the role that each of these two generations plays in next-generation preparation. Although I am using a dual-generation focus, in no way do I mean to imply that wealth creation is static. In other words, although a next-gen's parents may have created a meaningful amount of wealth, that inheritor could subsequently leverage the wealth and take it to a new level—or even go out and generate his or her own wealth without any funding from the parents.

Nor do I mean to suggest in any way that the parents of the present-generation wealth holder—the grandparents to the next generation, as that term is defined above—have no role in preparing the next generation of inheritors. In many cases grandparents are implicitly and sometimes explicitly involved in preparing their grandchildren.

Similarly, I do not mean to suggest that the children of the next generation of inheritors have no relationship to how their parents, aka the next generation, are prepared. Sometimes it is only when members of the next generation begin to have children of their own that they "wake up" and realize the importance of what their parents and grandparents had been modeling and sharing with them—or in some cases, the importance of doing something very differently than what their parents and grandparents did.

DEFINING PREPAREDNESS

Having defined whom we are referring to when we talk about next-generation preparation, we still need to define what we mean by preparation itself. Preparedness is sometimes referred to as *readiness*. It is incredibly important for parents, and also for advisors, to be able to answer the question, "What are we preparing them *for?*"

If you are a parent, take a minute now to complete the following statement: "I am preparing my children for . . ." If you are in the next generation, answer: "What am I being prepared for?" or "What am I preparing myself for?"

If you are not clear what you are trying to prepare for, then you reduce the odds that you will be successful in your efforts to create readiness! For example, if you want to prepare your child to become an electrician, then the path is relatively clear and focused (this assumes the child wants to be an electrician). Similarly, assuming the child desires it, to prepare your child to be an oncologist, the path is relatively clear and focused.

Specifically regarding the

It is incredibly important for parents, and also for advisors, to be able to answer the question, "What are we preparing them for?"

topic of finances, I have heard others advise, "Prepare your children for the amount of wealth you plan on transferring to them." I have always found this statement puzzling. It really provides no clues. Furthermore, it assumes that the amount of money to be inherited dictates the necessary preparation.

I have also heard, "Prepare your children to live as if they aren't going to inherit anything." This approach concerns me, as it could result in a sudden-wealth experience for the next generation—and this phenomenon can be destabilizing in different ways.

So what should we be trying to prepare our next generation for? To be good stewards of the wealth and legacy we will transfer to them? To be financially astute enough that they can manage their wealth? To lead happy, passionate, and productive lives?

Although I will now lay out the principles and practices that I have found to be most important that contribute to the successful preparation of the next generation, the answer to "What are we preparing them for?" is a personal decision, which is best guided by investment in our spiritual capital. In other words, our core values, overall life purpose—and more specifically, the purpose we assign to our wealth—and our faith can help each of us navigate this process in our own families.

This is another opportunity to fine-tune our personal *whys,* if we're parents, and as importantly allowing the next generation to fine-tune theirs.

PREPARATION IS A TWO-WAY STREET

Jordan (a financial advisor), Mr. and Ms. Smyth (his clients), and I were beginning to walk out of the conference room where we'd just had a thoughtful and productive meeting to plan for the imminent sale of the Smyths' company. During the meeting, we had talked about their spiritual capital (their values, purpose, and faith), the plan for the liquid wealth they were expecting from the sale, and their overall wishes for their young children's lives. Ms. Smyth and Jordan left the conference room first and were about five steps ahead of us when Mr. Smyth stopped, turned to me, and asked: "If you had to boil it down from your experience, what are the best practices you see other families institute to prepare their children for living with wealth? What would you say those are?"

Before I had a chance to think about my response, the following words flowed out of my mouth. "The families where the parents live happy and productive lives (not perfectly or without blemish), where their words align with their actions (authenticity), and they do not try to dictate their children's lives seem to have the best-prepared next generation."

Mr. Smyth said, "Thank you," and we walked out of the conference room.

As I reflect on that moment, my response did not provide any specific best practices; nevertheless, embedded in my imperfect response was a compilation of principles and practices that are found in family systems and happiness research, and come from the real-life practical wisdom I've gained from my work with clients during the many years I spent in the financial services industry, and the conversations I have had with educators, estate planners, and financial advisors. My response reflected the importance of the parents living and modeling happy and productive lives, *and* allowing their children to do the same. Next-generation preparation ideally is a two-way street.

As children move through the teenage, young adult, and adult stages in their lives, the responsibility for preparing the next generation in a family needs to shift incrementally to them. As children get older, parents need to dial down their involvement in their children's preparation. (Obviously this doesn't apply when there is a special needs child or a child with a substance abuse challenge.) Letting go of responsibility is not an either or scenario, just a necessary adaptation to align with the developmental opportunities in the next generation's lives. In other words, there needs to be a preparation "ownership shift" from one generation to the next. Like planning to transfer their wealth to their children, they need to plan for transferring the responsibility for preparation to their children as they move into adulthood.

More than once in my work with multiple generations of the same families, I've seen members of the wealth-creating, parental generation tend to parent like they run their companies: in a type-A manner. They typically set the agenda and expect others to follow their lead. They tend to come down on their children, and/or reduce their inheritance if the children fall out of alignment with their expectations. A child who continues to assert personal initiative that does not align with what his or her parents expect may be cast as a "problem child."

My training in family systems informs me that a so-called problem child (whom a psychologist would refer to as the "identified patient") is often a great source of information with which to understand a troubled family. This person represents what is not expected, so the child helps us understand what is expected and how the family manages the difference. The paradox in a family like this is that when someone from the next generation doesn't align with the parent generation they are discouraged, or to say the least, not supported. Yet, an important part of next-generation preparation is exactly this. Children need to carve out their own paths based on their passions, skills, and purpose (if it's a purpose they have chosen) and to be rewarded by their parents for doing so. For example, if a child determines that she is not passionate about the family business and decides to carve out her own professional path, this decision may at first disappoint a parent who hoped otherwise. However, this decision should communicate to the parents that their child is showing true growth and maturity, leading to a living positive legacy.

The ability to lessen their involvement in preparing the next generation doesn't seem to come easily to many parents, especially for entrepreneurial parents, who tend to have strong and persistent personalities and are used to having others following their directions. However, this is the greatest "work" of the parent generation in the preparation of the next generation. Parents will always be parents, yet when they have adult-age children they need to be able to converse more as peers (though not necessarily as equals).

Although this may not be an easy concept to accept, if you keep in mind that the fundamental existential nature of the parent-child relationship will always remain intact, you can see how the nature of the interaction needs to shift to two adults journeying through life together and sharing information and perspectives with one another.

When I talk to my dad, who is in his seventies, I still know and have deep feelings that he is my father. Sometimes I call him Dad, other times I call him Pops. But now when we talk, we are sharing our lives with one another as co-creators in the world. Over the last handful of years he has even said to me on more than one occasion, "Son, when we talk, I learn things from you." This doesn't change the fact that he is my dad and I am still his son.

WHICH MATTERS MOST: FINANCIAL IQ OR LIFE IQ?

Another, more conventional response I could have given to Mr. Smyth was, "Set up an allowance and budget for your younger children; for your older child, set up an investment account and have her begin to participate in the family foundation you plan to establish; and write a family mission statement." This response would have provided him with tactical best practices to follow, and in fact, these would have been helpful to the Smyth family.

The limitation of only providing this tactical advice, however, is that it really doesn't address the larger picture of next-generation preparation. Primarily, it places the focus on what the parent generation does to prepare the next generation.

Eighty-four percent of respondents to the PNC Wealth Management "Wealth and Values Survey," reported in January 2013, said that raising successful, hard-working children is their most important goal.[1] On a similar note, a 2012 survey of high net worth Americans, *U.S. Trust Insights on Wealth and Worth*, found that the number one reason parents did not disclose their wealth to their children was concern that "it will negatively affect their work ethic."[2] Based on these findings, maybe family advisors should host conferences with themes like: "How to foster a strong work ethic in the next generation?" or "Helping your clients define success and hard work for their families?"

Until advisors begin to provide best practices to meet the primary goals of many parents, for instance addressing the fear of raising children with affluenza, they won't be fully contributing to next-generation preparation. Increasing financial IQ is important and can contribute to financial responsibility and stewardship. Like the relationship between money and happiness, it alone doesn't ensure next-generation readiness.

An important element of our legacy to our children is contributing to their readiness. My preference is to frame this in terms of life maturity, or life IQ, if you will, rather than purely in terms of financial literacy or financial IQ. Life IQ is about having the knowledge, skills, and experience to flourish in any context; especially in the context of wealth. It is about understanding both the opportunities and responsibilities that come with wealth.

A wonderful depiction of increasing one's life IQ before one receives one's wealth can be found in the book, *The Ultimate Gift* by John Stovall (David C. Cook, 2001). The story depicts how the most important gifts we give to our heirs really have little to do with our financial wealth. In particular, the story reflects the importance of transferring or teaching gifts, such as friendship, learning, laughter, gratitude, and love, among others, before the wealth arrives.[3]

When surveyed by U.S. Trust on the topic of "At what age do you think your children will have the maturity necessary to handle the money they will receive?" 3 percent of respondents said at 18–24 years of age, 22 percent said 25–29, 48 percent said 30–39, and 28 percent said at 40-plus. Seventy-six percent agreed children need to be at least thirty to be mature enough to handle the wealth they will inherit.

Based on my own experience helping clients transfer their wealth, I would tend to concur with these findings. But although life IQ may have a positive correlation to age, this correlation isn't necessarily a direct or automatic correlation. We must bear in mind that one individual can have a higher life IQ at twenty-one than another at thirty-one. Our children's life IQs will be the product of a combination of information, parenting we give them, skills they develop, and what they are capable of as a result of their internal and external life experiences.

A few years back, I coached a successful entrepreneur and father named Devon. Devon was concerned about the lack of work ethic in his twenty-three-year old son. I learned that Devon and his wife had paid for their son's school, car, health insurance, and condo. After pointing out to Devon all the ways he had provided for his son, he stated, "Wow, we have really made it cushy for him, haven't we?" Unintentionally, Devon may have impeded his son's skill development by taking care of most of his needs and wants. Like Devon, many of us would be more successful in preparing the next generation if we followed the Chinese proverb: "Giving your son a skill is better than giving him one thousand pieces of gold.[4]

All parents want to provide for their children, and when there is an abundance of financial capital in a family they really can provide in very tangible ways. However, this common loving instinct especially needs to be kept in check if there is an abundance of financial capital. To borrow a term from Devon, when life is too cushy, or we try to help the caterpillar in its struggle to break out of its cocoon, we actually produce the opposite results we are intending.

Here again is a reason why investing into our spiritual capital is vitally important when preparing the next generation. We need to ensure that the spiritual dimension of our nature keeps the material dimension of our family resources in perspective. Loving our children does not equate to giving them everything we can, especially when providing for all of their needs, and many of their wants, may actually disempower them to live out their own legacies.

One of the natural instincts for parents is to provide a better life for their children, and if possible, for their grandchildren. This is a noble intent. However, for members of a generation that create significant wealth this noble intent may backfire. The unintended consequence of taking care of all or many of the next generation's needs and wants, especially during the formative young adult years, is the great potential to limit or lower their life IQ. Giving too much prevents young people from having the internal and external life experiences that are known to produce the very skills and traits that are necessary for long-term happiness and resilience. It removes the possibility of the personal growth that can result from taking responsibility for one's decisions *and* the results of those decisions, the confidence that increases as one sets goals and achieves them, and the self-knowledge and mastery that emerges from finding one's way through tough times and coming out on the other end stronger and wiser.

Another unintended consequence of providing the next generation with everything we can, especially if our children don't end up at a similar level of affluence we achieved, is their potential sense of being let down—especially when they become parents. In other words, they will not be able to maintain for themselves a lifestyle similar to the one we have, or provide a lifestyle similar to ours for their own children.

As an example, my client, Peter, and I were recently talking about how he was preparing his next generation and he confided that he felt concerned because it was statistically unlikely that his children would be able to create the wealth he had and he feared the long-term effects. Peter went on to say that he had provided special experiences for his children—things like private jets, great seats at different types of events, and travel to countries around the world—using his financial assets—and now he felt their experience in life was too one-sided. He was worried that they would feel impotent because they could not provide their own children with similar experiences.

This type of concern is common within families of wealth, especially for the generations closest to the wealth-creating generation. In some cases, next-generation family members will not even try to be productive in life, believing that will never be able to match the success of their parents. They are not sure how to get out from under the shadow of their parent's living legacy and create their own, even when the prior generation did not impose an unattainable standard. In other cases, the next generation is grateful for what their parents have provided, however, they decide to create a life and legacy based on their intelligence, talents, and hard work.

There is no panacea in next-generation preparation because no two families and no two children are alike. However, I will now present the core principles and practices that cut across all families to help increase the success of next-generation preparation, which is defined as both generations and the family as a whole, flourishing in whatever contexts they find themselves—especially in the context of wealth. And both generations are able to authentically live their intended legacies. This is really what legacy planning is about.

LIFE IQ: PRINCIPLES AND PRACTICES

Being clear on our values, purpose, and faith provides us a framework within which to navigate our individual and family lives. Having clear principles, or objectives, is important. Whether we are talking about next-generation preparation as parents or as children, the first principle we need to bring to bear on our situation is that of investing into our spiritual capital. How we do this, the practices we use, are highly individual.

When a family decides to invest together in their spiritual capital, it will help them identify their *shared* values, purpose, and faith. I highlight "shared" because it is unlikely that every family member will have the same exact values, purpose, and faith.

The second principle—and a practice that applies equally to parents and children—is having access to sound information. And specifically, because you are planning for a financial transfer, you will need information that increases your financial, estate, and tax acumen. There is a plethora of information in print and online to guide you. In addition to private research, I would recommend that you start your next-generation planning by meeting with the following professionals. Your:

- Wealth manager,
- Private banker,
- Financial planner,
- Family office principal,

- Accountant,
- Trust officer,
- Life insurance specialist,
- Property and casualty consultant, and/or
- Attorney.

These types of experts are able to help educate you and your family about their respective fields of knowledge. If you do not yet have one of the professionals just referenced, ask for a referral from a colleague, friend, or family member whom you respect and trust.

These two principles—investing in your spiritual capital and ensuring you have access to good financial information—will go a long way to improve your life IQ whether you are a parent or one of the next-gen. The remaining principles and practices I will offer on this topic are divided between ones that apply to members of the parental generation and ones that apply to the next generation.

Let's begin with the parents.

TEN PRINCIPLES AND PRACTICES FOR PARENTS TO RAISE THEIR CHILDREN'S LIFE IQS

Principle 1: Maximize your happiness.

Practice: Parents ask me all the time, "When should we start teaching our children about wealth?" My answer is, you have already begun to teach them through the way you live your lives, through the decisions you make, and the actions you take. Therefore, if you want to help ensure that your children live happy lives, model happiness in your life. Use Chapter 3 in this book as your guide.

Principle 2: Follow the platinum rule, it's not about you.

Practice: Let me say this again: It's not about you! All too often we assume others see the world the way we do. The traditional golden rule says, "Treat others as we would like to be treated." However, as parents, we need to live more by the platinum rule: "Treat others as *they* would like to be treated." Consider how each of your children sees the world before you make important decision for their lives.

To be even more concrete here in my advice, don't assume that the primary goal of the next generation is to steward your legacy and wealth. It is difficult to take ownership of something one didn't create oneself, especially if the parental messaging has been, "This is my/our wealth, not yours." Instead, direct your financial capital to serve your children's passion and purpose, and ultimately their legacy in the larger family story.

Principle 3: Distinguish between needs and wants.

Practice: Even though you may be able to provide for most of your children's needs and wants, don't! Instead, identify and stay focused on their true needs. Use their wants as teaching moments, as well as moments to bless them. But be clear on the difference.

Principle 4: Be the parent.

Practice: There is no substitute for your presence. Whether or not you want to be, you are a mentor and role model for your children. If you want to ensure that your children are prepared, make a personal investment in their lives. There is something about the parent-child relationship that ensures parents cannot be replaced by others. Having said this, investing in your children's lives will better equip you to determine who else should be in their lives as part of their development.

Principle 5: Be a coach.

Practice: No two children are the same. We see their unique temperaments emerge in the toddler years, if not sooner. Like great football coaches, create a system for running your offense and defense, and then coach each member of the team differently. Your quarterback will need something different from you than your defensive end, but both need to play the game within your overall system—at least until they create their own.

Principle 6: Be a storyteller.

Practice: One of the most powerful ways to teach children is through stories. Tell them stories about your family of origin, how you and your spouse met, the experiences you've had and people you've known who taught you the most, the start of the family business, and the vision you have for your family and your wealth. Be sure that your stories include both successes and failures, and also reveal the lessons learned from both.

In preparation for my meetings with multigenerational families, I ask each family member to bring a picture, song, and/or memento representing a story they believe should be communicated through the generations. Sharing these stories is usually one of the more powerful parts of the family meeting that ensues.

Principle 7: Be a giver.

Practice: Whether or not philanthropy is high on your value list, the giving of your time, talent, and treasures will be not only a blessing to others, it also will make you happier. If you want your children to lead happy lives, then modeling a life of giving will increase the chances that they, too, will live generously and feel happier.

Principle 8: Knowing a little psychology helps.

Practice: Financial wealth creates external and internal experiences. Commonly, when we think of financial wealth, we think of what it could provide us such as access, influence, and material objects. These are our external focuses. However, each family member also has a private, internal experience of wealth—and it may differ from that of other family members. Some members of a family may be very proud of their wealth. Others, a bit embarrassed. Some may view wealth as an opportunity to help people. Others, as an opportunity to spend on themselves. For those who initially create wealth it may bring a deep sense of accomplishment and reward. For those who inherit wealth it may bring a sense of insecurity and unworthiness. Never assume that everyone in your family feels the same way you do about your family's affluence.

Create conversations designed to get your family to reveal their internal experiences of wealth. For example, when sitting around the dinner table you could refer to someone you know or read about who has an abundance of wealth and describe this person. Then ask your family what they think this person could be experiencing inside as a result of wealth. Their answers may give you clues to what they are thinking or experiencing.

Principle 9: Be a perspective keeper.

Practice: Assuming you do not want the members of your family's next generation to have a view of the world skewed to affluenza—then, like Peter above, it is important to counterbalance their life experiences. If you want to take your family on luxurious vacations, for example, then also take vacations that have a limited budget within which all family members must operate. Ask your children to participate in deciding how to use the budget to plan the next family vacation.

If your children mostly socialize with others who have similar financial resources, then ensure that they form relationships with friends and/or extended family members who have less and more financial wealth then your family does. Create experiences that clearly bring to light whatever you believe needs to be counterbalanced.

I do not mean to imply in any way that members of affluent families should have guilt because of their wealth—not at all. This principle and practice best applies to parents who want to ensure that as part of their next-generation preparation their children develop a multidimensional perspective on the world.

Principle 10: Life IQ is about productivity, passion, purpose.

Practice: Being productive, following our passions, and knowing our purpose is important to our success in life. At the end of the day for wealth creators, success may be about fulfilling their passion and purpose. However, in a very literal way, their productivity is paramount to their accomplishments. This translates to long hours, hitting measurable goals, raising capital, generating enough revenue to pay employees, and possibly the creation of significant liquid wealth through a business sale.

It is less likely (although not impossible) for the next generation in an affluent family to be as productive as its predecessor. Therefore, it is important to ensure that the definition of being productive that a family collectively uses is broader than the one the wealth-creating generation demonstrated. If parents do not use a broader definition, they may unintentionally put their children on a path that leads to not even trying to be productive. This sometimes the case for next-gens who feel that the shadow of the prior generation is so big it is not even worth trying.

These principles and practices are part of a lifelong process of living out an intended legacy, and as a result, leaving the legacy we had hoped would be imprinted in our children's hearts and minds. As you will see, the principles and practices just discussed are not exclusive to parents, and have an overlap to the next generation's principles and practices.

Now, let's look at the set of ten principles and practices next-gen children can use to raise their own life IQ.

TEN PRINCIPLES AND PRACTICES FOR MEMBERS OF THE NEXT GENERATION TO RAISE THEIR LIFE IQ

Principle 1: Maximize your happiness.

Practice: Whether you are anticipating an inheritance or engaged in creating your own wealth, base your work, life, and relationships on your strengths, your passions, and your purpose to the greatest degree that you can. Let any financial capital you've inherited or created up to now serve them. Be sure to use Chapter 3 as your guide.

Also, please know that your parents want you to be happy; however, they don't always know how to ensure you are so they may try to put their definition of happiness on you. This is because they love you and want the best for you. It is important that you let them know how best to support you in your pursuit of happiness. Ultimately, we are responsible for our own happiness.

Principle 2: Adopt a first-generation mindset.

Practice: Whether you are in a generation that's two, three, or four beyond the generation that created significant wealth for your family is ultimately irrelevant to the decisions you make. No matter what kind of wealth your family controls, your life purpose is not necessarily to perpetuate the legacy of your parents, or to agree to live a life focused on stewarding someone else's wealth. Instead, learn to see yourself as a first-generation wealth creator who may or may not have material resources you can draw upon.

Your grandparents may have started out with one dollar, your parents with one hundred dollars, and you with a thousand dollars—but now you are still the first generation. You should be thinking, *Now that I have a thousand dollars, how do I maximize these resources not only to carry forward the family legacy, but also to have the greatest impact on future generations and contribute my part to the family legacy story?*

Create your own dream within the context of the larger family story—and pursue it wholeheartedly. If it aligns with your passions and purpose, then you could create even greater wealth than those who have come before you.

Principle 3: Distinguish between needs and wants.

Practice: You will find being part of a family with wealth, or as a wealth creator yourself, it is possible to take care of most, if not all of your material needs and wants the instant they arise. But do not! This can set you on a hedonic treadmill where you need more and more stimulation to glean the same level of joy from your possessions and experiences. Don't even get started in that direction; stay off the "treadmill" (unless you are exercising for your physical health).

Take care of your needs, and have fun deciding which wants you will meet. Being clear on your needs versus your wants will help you help your parents know how best to provide for you. It will also help you in your own financial management, and estate planning, and eventually in the parenting of your children.

Principle 4: Learn to be a good judge of character and competence.

Practice: We've discussed the importance of raising financial literacy to the preparation of your generation. If you plan to be an active advisor or leader in decisions related to one or more of your family's financial assets, then it is imperative that you develop a very high degree of competence in your area of responsibility (for example, investments). However, if this area doesn't pertain to your vocation, it is still important for you to cultivate a base level of financial skill in every area of your family's affairs, so that you can converse with family advisors and leaders, both inside and outside your immediate family.

One of the skills you want to hone is your ability to assess character and competence. When your wealth reaches a certain level, what is definite is that you and your family will depend on various advisors to help you operate, preserve, and grow the family's financial assets, at least part of which will be yours one day. Knowing enough to be able to assess a professional's competence (appropriate education, professional experience and savoir faire, understanding of the nomenclature and regulations), and character (integrity, intuition, high-caliber reputation, and appropriate references) is imperative.

Principle 5: Be adaptive and innovative.

Practice: Your family's wealth is likely to be represented by a number of family assets, among them houses, businesses, and investments, requiring that energy and resources be focused on keeping them going. In this scenario, it would not be uncommon for you to wonder where you fit in the family enterprises or what else you might need to do to keep things going smoothly. Entering the family business may seem like trying to get on a plane that has already started down the runway or is flying in midair. It is very important for your well-being, and for the sake of the larger family enterprise, to be able not only to adapt to the situation, but also to focus on how to be innovative. Maybe, you'll even decide you would prefer to get on another "plane" or build a plane yourself.

Allow the old adage "Necessity is the mother of invention" to be your guide. Innovation could apply to the process of taking the family business into the future or to creating a purposeful life outside of your family's enterprises. In either case, developing the skills of adapting and innovating is important to your preparation.

Principle 6: See obstacles and life trials as your friends.

Practice: For most people, life's trials contribute to stress and discomfort. As a result, they look for solutions to make their distress go away quickly. Having an abundance of financial resources expands the options for how to do so. This could mean by going on a spending spree, by physically removing oneself from a situation or relationship by traveling to another country, or by abusing a substance, such as alcohol or a narcotic.

It is important not to run from the trials in your life as these will provide you with the opportunity to grow and learn about yourself and others. Among other things, the ability to identify, assess, and control our emotions are significant aspects of emotional intelligence (EQ). A high EQ has been shown to contribute positively to many areas of personal and professional life.

Principle 7: Be a giver.

Practice: Whether or not you have access to your family wealth yet, you can give. Giving incorporates our time and talents as much as our treasures. As part of your pursuit of a happy life, it is important for you to contribute to other people's well-being. Get involved with groups whose work you believe in. If your family has a foundation, be part of the family giving. For example, you could help identify which organizations to give grants to. If there is an expectation that you will help direct the family foundation when the prior generation passes away, find out what the specific expectations are.

Principle 8: Knowing a little psychology helps.

Practice: Financial wealth creates external and internal experiences. Commonly, when we think of financial wealth, we think of what it could provide in our lives: access, influence, and material objects. Although this tends to have an external focus, each member of the same family may have a different internal experience of wealth. Some may be very proud of the wealth, and others a bit embarrassed. Some may feel excited because they see the wealth as an opportunity to help others, and others as an opportunity to spend it on themselves. For those who create the wealth, it may bring a deep sense of accomplishment and reward. For those who inherit it, it may bring a sense of insecurity and unworthiness.

Therefore, take an assessment of your internal experiences of your family wealth. It is not uncommon for inheritors to have mixed feelings about the inherited wealth, especially if it comes with a lot of strings attached. It is an important part of your preparation to make the inherited wealth your ally. Ensure that it serves your passions and purpose.

Principle 9: Know your parents are watching.

Practice: Your parents are watching you to see what decisions you make and actions you take, and whether you take responsibility for your life. The degree you do this is the degree they will feel you are prepared for what they want to share with you (both materially and otherwise). The more you turn to them to make decisions for you (as opposed to seeking their guidance), depend on their financial assets, and don't take responsibility for your actions, the less prepared they will imagine you are.

This practice is not about living an unblemished life or one that is based on meeting all your parents' expectations. The potential paradox is that the more you go to them to help you, the more they are likely to help, because this is the natural instinct of a parent. However, the cost of that help to you will be exactly what you (and they) do not want, that is, a life of dependency on others and their resources. Part of increasing your life IQ is about you preparing yourself.

Principle 10: Life IQ is about passion, purpose, and productivity.

Practice: As a next generation wealth holder, you may have advantages your parents didn't have when they were starting out in life. If one (or both) of your parents was the wealth creator in your family, rather than an inheritor, this parent is probably highly productive and possesses the character traits of extreme diligence and perseverance. If the only measure of productivity in a life were the amount of wealth that an individual created, then you might or might not stack up well against your parent. Productivity is paramount to wealth creators. As an inheritor, you must find your own way to define success in life. It may be first about passion and purpose, and only then productivity.

For many next gens who are happy, productivity is defined by how much they are able to build a life and work around their passion and purpose; especially if they don't have to worry about making the money to cover their lifestyle. A classic example of this is the next generation family member who after inheriting five, ten, or twenty million dollars decides to be a grade school teacher or to work full time volunteering with a charitable organization. Of course, it is also possible that the next generation is able to take their inheritance or family business and multiply its returns.

COMMUNICATION

Everyone acknowledges the importance of effective communication. And it is. Yet, families rarely talk specifically about their finances to each other. There are a plethora of resources on communication skills, and if you believe you, or your family, need to improve these skills, please seek them out.

That being said, in my experience the reason wealth holders don't talk about money with the next generation has less to do with their communication skills and more to do with the implications of others knowing about their wealth, such as fearing their children will develop affluenza or be taken advantage of by predatory individuals. Some believe that one is not supposed to talk about money, that, for instance, it's crass.

However you personally feel about having money conversations within your family, please remember that two-way communication is crucial to next-generation preparation. Here are a few guidelines that can be used to prepare your family to talk about money.

- *Don't talk about the money.* I have found that the number one stumbling block to communication is that wealth-holding parents assume they have to talk about their actual financial statements. You don't have to talk about the actual money—the dollars and cents of things—for some time.

There is a lot to talk about before getting to the financial statement.

Out of all the families I've ever worked with, I can count on one hand how many parents revealed the actual details of their financial picture and estate plan to the entire family. In all these cases, the next generation was, on the low end, in their thirties. Most were in their forties or older.

It is most important to talk with the next generation about the responsibilities, opportunities, and expectations that come with wealth, at least until much later in their lives—unless, of course, there is an unforeseen early death of a key decision maker. Then a different formula for family wealth governance will be required. From the perspective of the next generation, it is critical to focus on the principles for raising their life IQ. It is not essential to know the exact amount of their inheritance before completing college, for example. Once they begin seriously pursuing a vocation and move toward marrying and creating families of their own, they benefit from having a greater understanding of their potential inheritance so that this information can be factored into their own legacy planning. In many families with an abundance of financial assets, prenuptial agreements are expected practices, therefore getting married tends to be a common catalyst for more detailed wealth discussions.

- *Get clear on your legacy message.* For parents, communicating about the family's wealth to the next generation is more about getting the message right. The message refers to the shared values, purpose, and expectations of the family. Staying on message is important whether a conversation is taking place within a family of origin or with a spouse, significant other, extended family member, or a friend. More specifically, use the questions from family members pertaining to money or stories in the news pertaining to money as teachable moments.

• *Move toward transparency.* I don't want to promote keeping secrets or denying what really is, however this doesn't have to equal full financial transparency all at once. Instead, it is an intentional, artful process to know when, where, and to whom to reveal the fuller financial picture. In order to prepare the next generation for a happy life and personal fulfillment in the context of the wealth they have inherited or will one day inherit, the two generations of a family need to engage in ongoing, two-way communication.

As a parent, you can set the stage and parameters for your family to talk about its broader wealth, using a statement such as: "Family, we have worked really hard and, as a result, have been able to create financial wealth that allows us to take care of most, if not all, of our needs, and some of our wants. As we have discussed, we believe that having financial wealth brings both opportunities and responsibilities. Preparing ourselves and future generations for the opportunities and responsibilities of wealth is very important to us, and is a lifelong process. Therefore, I want us to maintain open communication through the years, not only about our financial capital, but all our other forms of capital, too. Please trust us that we will share more details of our finances over time, as we are ready and you are ready, so that we can all plan for success together."

A number of years ago I was conducting a family meeting. Seated around the table were the matriarch (mom), patriarch (dad), several of their adult children, and a couple of trusted advisors. At this point in the patriarch's life he had created a successful financial enterprise. During one of the discussions, he began to overtly express his frustrations with his children, saying that they weren't fully appreciating what he had done for them.

I waited for the right opening, and then said to the patriarch, "It must be frustrating that you can't take your forty-plus years of professional experience and learning and just pour it into your children's minds. Frustration about this is a common experience for successful entrepreneurs like you." This statement must have accurately described what the man was feeling and normalized his experience, because his frustration seemed to evaporate. The rest of the conversation shifted to the theme we have been exploring in this book: Next-generation preparation is multidimensional and multigenerational.

Let's revisit the question of how to define readiness to receive transferred wealth.

What are you trying to prepare the next generation in your family for—to be good stewards of the wealth and legacy you have created? To be sufficiently astute financially so that they can manage your wealth? To lead happy, passionate, and productive lives?

As someone in the next generation being prepared for wealth transfer, do you know and understand the significance of what you are being prepared for? How are you preparing yourself?

I don't know what your family's answer is to "What are we preparing for?" but I do know that if you follow the principles and practices I've outlined in this chapter you will significantly increase the chance that the transfer happens successfully.

Before you turn to the next chapter, take some time to assess how you are doing in regard to these principles and practices. Continue to implement the practices in areas where you are proficient and invest more time in developing additional practices that you know can make a difference in your family's next-generation preparation.

CHAPTER SIX
GIVING AND SHARING

*"Let us not be satisfied with just giving money. Money is not
enough, money can be got, but they need your hearts to love them.
So, spread your love everywhere you go."*
—Mother Teresa

If I asked you to define philanthropy, what would you say? What
is commonly understood by the word "philanthropy" is the
practice of affluent people (and also corporations) giving away
some portion of their money.

Giving away wealth can bring great good to individuals and
communities, not to mention joy to the one who gives. The most
notable example of philanthropic intentions is the Giving Pledge.
Responding to a campaign launched in 2010 by Warren Buffet
and Bill and Melinda Gates, 100-plus billionaires have committed to give at least half of their wealth to charities during their
lifetimes or after their deaths.[1] This pledge has been described as
a moral commitment rather than as a binding legal contract. Bill
Gates, one of the first billionaires to make this pledge, at one time

reportedly said, "Is the rich world aware of how four billion of the six billion live? If we were aware, we would want to help out, we'd want to get involved."[2]

How an individual and family decide to give and share their resources is one of the five most important family wealth decisions they can make. This decision has a direct impact on our living legacy; therefore we need to plan for it accurately.

What I have been observing in my work with individuals and families is a trend toward not waiting until one is at retirement age, has finished accumulating wealth, or dies before actively integrating philanthropy in their lives. Younger generations, in particular, view philanthropy as a way to express a greater purpose and meaning in life, a faster means to make an impact on the world and produce a positive legacy. An article published by *Knowledge@Wharton,* the online business journal of the Wharton School, identified this trend, saying, "For younger donors, it's not only about giving money. I think there is a growing sense that the solutions to social problems are going to come from active engagement with nonprofits—from contributing expertise, knowledge, and networking. The question is, what else you can do besides write a check or write a check that clears after you're dead?"[3]

"What else can you do besides write a check?" What kind of question is this? Doesn't philanthropy require money?

I have a friend, her name is Lynn. For most of her life, Lynn has lived paycheck to paycheck. Yet she is one of the most generous people I know. Lynn takes from her limited resources and gives to those in need. On the other hand, I have worked with individuals who, by any standard, have an abundance of financial capital, yet don't feel they have enough to actively give it to others just yet. These types of experiences have led me many years ago to think more deeply about what it means to be philanthropic.

Etymologically, the word *philanthropy* refers to the love of humanity or promoting the welfare of others. A few of the many synonyms for philanthropy are "charity," "compassion," and "generosity." Given this truer definition, when speaking with my clients I have found it useful to minimize the use of the word *philanthropy*, which in our culture tends to apply to only one dimension of giving—gifts of financial capital—and instead say, "Giving and sharing with others." This language incorporates financial capital even as it allows us to embrace a multidimensional understanding of philanthropy. This framework incorporates the giving and sharing of all our capitals: the financial, intellectual, social, human, and spiritual. Furthermore, this framework allows everyone to see themselves as, and actually be, philanthropists, not just those with extraordinary financial abundance.

There is another subtler, and more challenging dimension to philanthropy that is reflected in the quote at the start of this chapter. This dimension was pointed out to me by one of my clients. I was leading his family, the Wrights, through the same values exercise I described in Chapter 4. After each family member identified his or her core values, I asked the family member to read out loud his or her respective list of top values. After a number of the family members read off their lists, the word *philanthropy* was referenced a few times.

Now it was time for Mr. Wright to read his list aloud. He read a few of his values and then put down the cards that were in his hand, and said, "I wanted to choose philanthropy like some of you did. However, I think too many people give away their money for tax benefits or really don't have any personal connec-

> Everyone can be a philanthropist, not just those with extraordinary financial abundance.

tion to the impact of their philanthropic giving. So I have chosen the value words *generosity* and *compassion* because I believe they better reflect an attitude of a giving heart."

The epitome of giving from a place of love—that is, an agape or spiritual type of non-romantic love—is portrayed early in the iconic Victor Hugo novel *Les Miserables*. Bishop Myriel has provided shelter to a former convict, Jean Valjean, who has recently been released from prison for stealing. In the middle of the night, Valjean steals the bishop's silverware and runs away. He is caught by the police and brought back to face the Bishop. However, the bishop rescues him by claiming that the silverware was a gift. At that point, he gives Valjean two additional silver candlesticks and chastises him in front of the police for leaving in such a rush that he forgot these most valuable pieces.

How counterintuitive is Bishop Myriel's response? Does he not have every right to have Jean Valjean pay a price for stealing from him, especially after he took him into his home and provided him shelter? For those who know this story, that specific experience begins the transformation of Valjean's life. Toward the end of *Les Miserables* there is a line that sums up the fuller definition of philanthropy: "To love another person is to see the face of God."[4]

If one aspires to leave a positive legacy, the hidden key that makes this possible is the nature of the decisions we make regarding giving and sharing all our capitals via love. This understanding of philanthropy can transform our philanthropic acts, so instead of thinking of giving and sharing like Bill Gates did, "Is the rich world aware of how four billion of the six billion live?" we could say, "Potentially, there are six billion philanthropists in this world."

I am not being naïve. Gifts of money matter greatly to those in need who receive them. However, statistically there are abundantly more people like my friend Lynn who live paycheck to paycheck, yet have the potential to leave a legacy that positively transforms the lives around them, than there are billionaires. Like the act of Bishop Myriel, it only takes one gift of love to begin to transform to the life of another.

Similar to all important decisions we and our families will make throughout our lives, investment in our spiritual capital is the best GPS to guide what we give, to whom we give it, and when will we give and share it. In the remainder of this chapter, I will provide various illustrations of giving and sharing, though these examples are not meant to determine for you and your family how you choose to be philanthropists. How you choose to be philanthropic is your personal decision.

THE GIVING AND SHARING PROCESS

The idea of giving involves how we give to, and nurture ourselves. For the purpose of this discussion, however, I am defining the giving process as one that involves at least two parties: the individual or family (or family business) that decides to give and share, and the individual, family, or organization that receives the gift. These are the direct parties involved.

Now, they may not be the only parties involved. For example, when I give or share any of my capitals with my wife, there is the potential that my children will experience something consciously or unconsciously as a result. I will speak in extremes to illustrate this point.

If I choose to ignore my wife, never celebrate her birthdays, and rarely, if ever, bring her gifts of gratitude, our children are likely to witness this and form an internal impression of how to relate to another person (in this case, quite selfishly). On the other hand, if I publically express my love and admiration for my wife, set up big birthday celebrations for her, and adorn her with gifts, our children are likely to have a very different impression of how to conduct relationships.

In these polar examples, our children are not involved in the direct giving or sharing. But they are experiencing ripple effects from how my wife and I give and share with one another.

When an individual or a family chooses to give and share capitals with others, it not only has the potential to benefit the direct receivers of those gifts, it can also inspire and give hope to people who are aware of expressions of generosity and compassion. A little bit of radiance rubs off from the lamp they light. When I learned that Rick Warren, author of *The Purpose Driven Life,* after attaining significant wealth from the sales of this book, decided to become what he refers to as a *reverse-tither*—meaning he gives away 90 percent of his earnings and lives on 10 percent—my wife and I were inspired to increase our giving as we create more wealth.

Imagine what the multiplying effect of giving and sharing would be throughout the world if people everywhere realized they all have the potential to be philanthropists.

In my family, we are intentional about our giving, and our giving includes all our capitals. Even though the entire family participates in one way or another in giving and sharing, my wife wears the title of Director of Giving in our household. We both believe the day-to-day practice of giving and sharing with others is not only the right thing to do, but also a great way to prepare our children for productive and happy lives in the future. The value we aim to embody in our choices is reflected in the biblical passage, "From everyone who has been given much, much will be demanded" (Luke 12:48). Because we do not only interpret this as referring to our financial capital, we have explained to our children that we should not only share our material blessings with others, but also our time, love, and kindness.

I once heard someone say, "Give until it hurts." I don't believe this expression best describes the process and outcome of giving through love. I understand how, when we feel we don't have gas left in the tank and a friend or family member asks for time and energy, it requires us to take a deep breath and muster up the energy to be present and pay attention. However, in most cases, when we do this, we actually find our gas tanks filling up again. It is paradoxical how this works. I also understand that it can feel scary to give financially to others when we are not sure we have all our financial goals securely met, yet when we do, once again we somehow experience an intrinsic reward and the bills continue to get paid. So I don't think the proper expression is "Give until it hurts." I'd rather say, "Give until it feels good."

As we explored in Chapter 3, giving is an important practice that contributes much to our pursuit of happiness. By way of reminder, a study found that in almost every country around the world, when someone had the choice to spend money on himself or herself, or on someone else, and they chose someone else, they were happier.[5]

I recently attended a leadership teleconference at which John C. Maxwell spoke. As I was jotting down some notes, one statement Maxwell made in reference to the attributes of great leaders caused me think about the legacy of leaders. To paraphrase, he said that great leaders wake up every day and think about *how they can add value to the lives of others.*[6] This is an excellent practice to adhere to for becoming a great philanthropist.

An important practice for a giver is to distinguish between the golden rule and the platinum rule of giving I mentioned in Chapter 5. I believe both rules are necessary depending on the opportunity and the receiver, and do not view them as mutually exclusive.

As a reminder, the golden rule for giving reflects the process by which givers first identify their own values, passions, and interests and then give to others in a way that aligns with these. For example, two important goals of my family's giving are that we focus on children and meeting their basic needs, such as food, clothing, and shelter. Therefore, people and organizations that focus on these objectives are likely to be places where we will give and share our different capitals.

The platinum rule of giving is a process whereby givers first identify the needs of the receiver and then channel their giving to meet the receiver's needs. For example, my wife and I recently went to one of the organizations we give to with an idea for how we wanted to help. The woman who was the director of this particular organization very graciously said, "Thank you for your generosity. However, there is a greater need we are trying to solve here at the organization." At first, my wife, the Director of Giving, was a little let down because she had been very excited with the idea we brought to the organization. But it only took a couple of minutes for her to feel grateful that in some small way we were able to meet the actual need of the receiver of our gifts.

It is especially important to consider the impact of a gift on a receiver when the receiver is a person rather than an organization. To the best of our abilities we must try to anticipate the potential consequences of our sharing, for better or worse. Will the gift enhance the receiver's life, contribute to his or her overall well-being, and lead to the fulfillment of the receiver's dreams? Or might a gift unintentionally hinder or dampen the receiver's life? Following the platinum rule of giving helps mitigate unintended negative impacts and maximizes positive impacts.

TIME, TALENT, AND TREASURES

The personal attorney of a high-profile professional athlete and his wife asked me to consult with them. Our first meeting was in a private room in a restaurant in New York City. During the meeting, the wife expressed how she wanted to give away more of their money to various charities. For his part, her husband was quite reluctant to give much money away. He said, "I don't know how long my professional sports career will last, so I don't want to start giving away our money yet."

I asked the couple if they had been participating in fundraising for any charities. Fifteen minutes later, after listening to example after example of how they have helped raise funds for others, it was clear that they were quite philanthropic. The challenge for this couple was that they had a limited understanding of what philanthropy meant. They, like others, understood their philanthropic efforts primarily as giving away their money. Yet this professional athlete raised a lot of money for others just by signing various memorabilia that were then auctioned and giving speeches. He helped various boards of directors raise money by participating in their charitable events. I pointed out that they were already quite philanthropic in terms of their time and talents, in addition to their financial "treasure." This framework gave them a new way of being philanthropic and, as a result, they felt greater harmony and alignment in their relationship.

Following this conversation, the couple decided to empower the wife by setting aside a giving budget that would allow her to give money directly when she felt moved to do so, instead of the family's philanthropy happening primarily through the efforts of her husband.

Some of the families I have worked with expect that some portion of their giving must involve their time and direct involvement in the charities they give to financially. The next-generation offspring of one my client families recently met together without their parents to strategize various ways they could collaborate by giving their time and talents to charities in addition to whatever financial giving they were already doing as individuals. This exercise enhanced their teamwork and decision-making skills.

I coauthored a paper with Hannah Shaw Grove and John Morris, entitled "Purposeful Travel," which highlights the different ways a family can travel together and build trips around a purpose other than just visiting a desired location. One of the examples we provide is designing a trip around the purpose of giving back. Here is an excerpt from this paper.

The effect on children of traveling for philanthropic purposes can be profound. They will meet children their own age living in starkly different circumstances. This personal experience can help them understand what life is really like for billions of people subsisting in developing countries. Giving children a role in uplifting those less financially fortunate can awaken their minds to the harsh realities of the developing world, but also empower them as to what they can do for others and why this is important.

You can demonstrate to your children that philanthropy and purposeful travel go hand-in-hand. You can help children develop the habit of giving when planning a trip by having them consider what they can contribute or what they can give back to the destination that they are visiting. Purposeful travel can teach children to ask "Who can we help next summer?" rather than "Where can we go next summer?"[7]

GIVING AND SHARING OF ALL OUR CAPITALS

As the aforementioned *Knowledge@Wharton* article states, being a philanthropist often includes "contributing expertise, knowledge, and networking."[8] These attributes fit nicely into our FISHS framework.

- *Expertise* is an element of our human capital
- *Knowledge* is an element of our intellectual capital
- *Networking* is an element of our social capital

I believe the FISHS framework enables us to see ourselves as philanthropists, and thereby as having the capital necessary to contribute to a positive legacy. Whether or not people have an abundance of financial capital, each person has all the other capitals to give and share, and our spiritual capital in particular helps us to pursue the type of love that Bishop Myriel demonstrated. Our spiritual capital empowers us to give and share from a place of love.

Let's take another tour of each of the capitals in turn, beginning with financial capital, and look at examples of how we can give and share what we possess for the betterment of others and the world at large.

Financial giving. There are many examples of individuals, families, and corporations that give financial capital, and thank goodness for them. One of the newer trends in the area of financial giving is microfinancing, funding tiny loans to small business owners, usually located in developing nations, who lack access to traditional banking services. The idea is to help people lift themselves out of poverty.

One family I know has set up a family foundation. Each child is encouraged to participate in age-appropriate ways to the foundation. For example, the younger children are asked to conduct research on charities they would like the foundation to contribute to. They then present their recommendations to the foundation's board of directors. Adult children are asked to rotate board membership, thereby giving each the opportunity to make important decisions regarding how much and to which charities the foundation contributes. These practices contribute to the family's ability to make decisions together, teach the younger children critical thinking and presentation skills, and give the older children the opportunity to exercise their leadership skills.

Another family has a similar set up, however they've added one other component. The parents match any financial contribution their children make to the foundation up to a certain dollar figure.

Yet another family doesn't have a family foundation, yet wants to contribute to similar outcomes as those just referenced. The parents set aside a certain giving budget each year for their three teenage and young adult children. They give each child the same dollar amount (for example, $1,500) to contribute and ask them to identify charities they would like to support. The children then present their proposals to their parents before the money is released. Another $3,000 is given collectively to all four children to give away. These giving strategies are helping their children build important skills that are vital to the success of the family and their own evolving legacies.

Intellectual giving. Intellectual capital reflects our life's resume. It consists of the formal and informal education we've received, combined with our perspectives and based on our unique life experiences. Setting aside time to tutor or mentor others in the areas we know a lot about is a great way to give and share intellectual capital.

I have worked with many people who come from a financially abundant background who have decided to leverage their wealth so they can give back to the community by teaching in an inner city. Although the pay is low, their basic lifestyle expenses are covered. Their inherited family wealth enables them to choose this lifestyle.

Another example of giving and sharing intellectual capital is to intentionally make ourselves available to others by providing coaching and mentoring to people in subject areas we know something about.

Social giving. Our social capital refers to the networks of relationships of which we are a part. And remember, our social networks are connected to other people's social networks through relationships. Therefore, within our network of relationships is a vast amount of resources. I am reminded of a situation in which someone was diagnosed with a disease that required special attention. This person's parents reached out to their network where someone fortunately knew someone else who was able to get them an appointment with a well-known doctor who specialized in this particular disease.

There are innumerable examples of people introducing other people to one another for the purposes of business (referrals), dating (matchmaking), and collaboration (for example, for the cause of fundraising). An extraordinary amount of personal and professional connectivity is taking place worldwide now through online social networks. A few years back I was connected to someone on LinkedIn regarding a business opportunity. Now he and his wife are two of my closest, most trusted friends and colleagues.

Human giving. Human capital refers to each person's strengths, talents, and passions. Identifying these and then building a life around them contributes to our lasting happiness. In addition, knowing other people's strengths, talents, and passions can help us plan for transferring our wealth to them. In other words, it's the platinum rule. We can ask ourselves if giving and sharing supports their strengths, talents, and passions, and is not based on our expectations of what their strengths, talents, and passions should be?

For people who are very good with their hands, volunteering time to build a house for Habitat for Humanity may be a good opportunity for human giving, as would be helping a neighbor with a building project. For people with strong analytical minds, helping someone else make an important business decision can be of great value to that person.

The heart of building a high-performing team is knowing what are each person's strengths, talents, and passions. Most team structures depend on the differing strengths, talents, and passions of their members being combined to attain a goal.

Spiritual giving. Our spiritual capital not only helps us navigate our important decisions, such as the decision to give, it also helps us do things like good works even when we don't feel up to it, and enables us to have a greater sense of contentment, which in turn enhances our ability to relate better to others.

Even if, in our eyes, the receiving party has not quite earned our gift, tapping into the Divine gives us the courage and strength to give in love (what we call *agape*) despite ourselves. Another of the subtler and more challenging aspects of giving and sharing can involve gifting to those we haven't forgiven, such as a family member with whom we are in conflict. Such challenging gifting can give us the grace to forgive and mend fences.

This type of compassionate, spiritual giving is not always easy, but if we can demonstrate the giving nature of Mother Teresa or Bishop Myriel it takes our giving to another dimension and expands the reach of our intended living and lasting legacy.

INTENTIONAL RANDOM ACTS OF KINDNESS

My wife came home one day after going to the grocery store. Her face was glowing as she began to share the following story with me. She said, "I was in the process of loading the food items from my cart onto the counter when I heard the lady in front of me talking with the cashier. This lady sounded stressed. She was telling the cashier something about losing her coupons and not having enough money with her." Without giving it much thought, my wife said to the cashier, "I would like to pay for her groceries." The cashier seemed confused by the offer. So did the woman who had lost her coupons, who said to my wife, "Why would you pay for my groceries? Who are you? No one ever does things like this."

My wife said, "I would like to."

After the transaction was done, the woman said, "I have to call my husband and tell him what you did."

Then my wife said, "You now have a new story to tell him," meaning as a substitute for telling him the stress of losing her coupon story.

Coincidentally, while my wife was in the parking lot loading her car with our groceries, she heard the woman telling someone else, ". . . and she bought my groceries." This woman had already begun to tell her new story.

I never asked my wife how much she paid for the woman's groceries because it does not matter. It could have been twenty dollars or two hundred dollars. What matters was that my wife intentionally engaged in a random act of kindness. This tiny act of giving apparently made a big impact on the woman she helped. My wife never saw this woman again, but we like to imagine that, in some small way, this woman's life was positively impacted and maybe, just maybe, as a result, it had a positive impact on others as a result. Perhaps one day the woman will return the favor by doing a kindness for someone else.

Caine Monroy was a nine-year old boy who spent weekends at the store of his father, George, which was located in East Los Angeles. Because of the store's location it had little foot traffic. In an attempt to help his dad make money, Caine decided to build an arcade of games in front of the store made out of cardboard boxes. Caine was quite industrious, creative, and entrepreneurial. He built and designed all the arcade games himself. The various games were cut out of the cardboard boxes and taped together. He also created a ticket and prize-redemption system, using some of his old toys as prizes. Certain games required him to literally enter the back of the cardboard box to push the winning tickets through a cut-out slot. Very few people entered the store, so Caine had few customers in his arcade. Yet he never lost faith or enthusiasm.

Then one day, Nirvan Mullick entered the store to get a part for his car. He decided to play the arcade games and was blown away by Caine's level of commitment and passion for the arcade. As a result, Nirvan decided to make a documentary about Caine, which he called *Caine's Arcade.* Using various social media outlets, in coordination with Caine's dad, Nirvan created a flash mob to come to the store and play in the arcade as a way to raise money for both Caine and George's store. The eleven-minute video went viral via Vimeo, YouTube, and other video sites. It had two million views in four days[9] and inspired many people around the world.

Since Nirvan shared his time and talents with Caine (and indirectly with his father) via the flash mob and documentary, hundreds of thousands of dollars have been raised, various contests held, and awards given around the world. Caine Monroy has made numerous high-profile speaking engagements. This is truly an inspirational story of how Caine's human, intellectual, and spiritual capitals, combined with Nirvan's intellectual, human, social, and spiritual capitals, were exponentially multiplied and produced financial capital as well as creating a legacy that still inspires many people today.

Like Nirvan Mullick and my wife, are you ready to intentionally do random acts of kindness for your family members, people at your workplace, or at the grocery store? Do you wake up every day, thinking, "How can I add value to the lives of others?" I trust that after reading this chapter you are. I also hope you have a greater understanding of the various ways you can give and share not only your financial capital, but also every other form of capital you possess. All of us have the potential to be great philanthropists and contribute to the positive legacy of ourselves and others. So please remember, your legacy starts today. It's not about what we leave at the end of our lives, but how we choose to live every moment of our lives that makes a real, enduring difference.

CHAPTER SEVEN

TAKING CARE OF THE BUSINESS OF THE FAMILY

"Other things may change us, but we start and end with the family."
—Anthony Brandt

Edna, in her late seventies when we spoke, had lost her husband unexpectedly many years earlier, due to a sudden heart attack. When her beloved husband died, not only did Edna lose the love of her life and best friend, but also the person who'd built and run their family business. She teared up as she told me how wonderful he was. As we spoke at length about her family, Edna described her two grown children, a son and a daughter. As younger people, both had worked for the family business. At the time of his father's death, the elder child, Steve, had bought it from his mother and was still running it.

As she was giving me the details, Edna leaned forward and in a soft voice said, "The business hurt our family."

"How so?" I asked.

"My children used to be close," she replied. "They are cordial with one another now, but I know something has come between them—and that it happened when my husband died. When he passed, we didn't have a plan for who would take over the business. At the time, my daughter, Sonia, was not working in the business. I have come to learn in recent years that she had always hoped one day to return to it. Steve, who was more qualified, took over. He stated from the very beginning that he didn't want any other family members working in the business. Since then, I have adjusted my estate plan so that Sonia will receive a larger sized inheritance to make the situation seem fairer. However, I am brokenhearted that my children are not as close as they once were, and that our family legacy has been tainted."

I asked Edna if she and her children had ever spoken about the decisions that were made regarding the family business when her husband died, and she said, "No. His death happened so fast that I simply tried to do the best I could at the time."

When I later spoke to Sonia directly about what she referred to as "our *former* family business," she said, "Not only am I not allowed to work in what was my father's business, but neither can my children. This will prevent my children from being part of my father's legacy." When I spoke to Steve he said he believed he'd made the best decision for the long-term success of the business.

Regrettably, the story of this family's lack of communication and hurt feelings is not unique. A family business can function unintentionally as a magnifying glass to intensify the family's existing dynamic. The decisions made for the purpose of doing business can be catalysts for distance, stress, and outright conflict among family members. These types of unintended family dynamics not only hurt members of the family, they also have the potential to undermine the success of the family business. It doesn't matter how small or large your business is, or how many people you employ to operate it. In their book, *Family Wars* (Kogan Page, 2010), Grant Gordon and Nigel Nicholson provide numerous similar cautionary tales of family dysfunction, showing how conflicts have

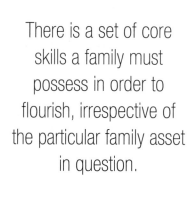

There is a set of core skills a family must possess in order to flourish, irrespective of the particular family asset in question.

even impacted some of the largest, most effective, and financially successful family run companies in the world, including Koch Industries, Gallo Family Vineyards, and Guinness and Company.[1]

This chapter covers the last of the five most important areas of family wealth decision-making that contribute to our living and lasting legacy, the family owned business. As with every other important family wealth issue addressed in this book, the *whys* that will guide your decisions in your business—which are hopefully guided by your spiritual capital—can only be answered by you and your family. These particular decisions focus squarely on how family members plan for, and equip themselves to work together in the context of a family business or share any family asset, such as a family foundation.

As reflected later on in the chapter, there is a set of core skills a family must possess in order to flourish, irrespective of the particular family asset in question. Initially, I will focus my comments primarily on families with a privately held business.

In the lifespan of a family business, many decisions are made. These answer questions such as:

- What is our succession plan?
- Shall we invest further in the business in order to expand our offerings and reach?
- Shall we sell the business?
- Can any family member own company stock whether or not this individual works in the business?
- What are the guidelines for a family member who wants to enter the business, especially in a leadership role?

These types of decisions are typically associated with the area of family governance. Family governance pertains to how the family and non-family members make decisions together, in this case, about the family business. However, effective decision making also requires other skills, such as trust and communication, which are not traditionally classified as aspects of family governance. Just as they do when approaching the other important decisions covered in this book, people too often approach the decisions they need to make for their family run businesses one-dimensionally, like Steve. In addition to finance, there are other, very important dimensions that also contribute to the success of a family in the context of a business. We will review these together later in this chapter.

THE FAMILY BUSINESS

In my research on family members who work together in business, I have found that when the family system functions at a high level it has a positive impact on the overall business system, including on the non-family members who work in the business. When the family system functions at a low level, it has a negative ripple effect on the overall business system. Thus, when family members function well together in their business, the business has a greater chance of being successful. When the family does not function well together, it has the potential to cause the disso-lution of the business.

A couple of years back, I attended the Family Firm Institute Conference, which focused specifically on family businesses. There I heard John A. Davis, Ph.D., a professor from Harvard Business School, share similar findings as mine. He said, "After thirty years of experience, I have found that the family system is the fundamental link to the stability and performance of the family business."[2]

The succession statistics among family businesses are dis-mal. The Family Business Institute website reports that about 30 percent of family businesses survive being put into the hands of the second generation, 12 percent remain viable into the third generation, and only about 3 percent of family businesses op-erate into the fourth generation or beyond.[3] Although there are many reasons for the dismal succession rate (including that de-scendants of the original creators of these businesses have dif-ferent talents and interests than their forbearers and choose not to work in ways they don't enjoy), most of the professionals who work in the family business consulting and coaching field, like myself, agree that interpersonal dynamics among family mem-bers plays a significant role in whether or not a family business continues. If members of a family get along, they enjoy working together. If they don't, they prefer to separate. Or, if a family lead-er in the business believes that a decision pertaining to the busi-ness may cause hurt feelings or lead to conflict between family members, this decision may be avoided or compromised, result-ing in a missed or poorly managed opportunity for the business.

The good news is that there are families whose members are capable of working together and succeeding both as families and as business partners. Some family businesses proactively plan to transfer ownership of the business to future generations. For example, Barone Ricasoli Winery, the oldest winery in Italy, was founded in 1141 and is still family owned. The present owner represents the thirty-second generation of the family.

The decision of whether or not a child is to succeed a parent as the leader of a family owned business can be one of the toughest decisions, especially if the company operates on a very large scale. Consider the well-known global family enterprise Marriott International, which was founded in 1927. Recently, the eighty-five-year old enterprise appointed its first non-family CEO. The preceding CEO, Bill Marriott, a son of the founder, had four children. Of these, John was a likely candidate to succeed his father as CEO. He had worked in nearly every part of the business over a thirty-year period. After intentional planning with open communication, including input from the board of directors whose chief responsibility is to the stockholders, for the betterment of the enterprise, current CEO Arne Sorenson was appointed instead.

In detailing how he came to his decision to name a non-family member as his successor for an article in *Harvard Business Review*, Bill Marriott said, "John performed very well in all those roles. He worked extremely hard, and he knew the business from A to Z. I was determined to mentor him and to give him all the tools he would need to succeed. But as he moved from running hotels to working at headquarters, he seemed less happy. . . . As I watched John adapt to this role, I could see that he wasn't having much fun. . . . But the more I looked at the situation, the more I realized that John is a natural born entrepreneur. He doesn't have the temperament to run a company the size of Marriott today. . . . Over time we both came to the conclusion that, wonderful as it would have been for me to hand Marriott off to my son, he wasn't the right choice. . . . Although I miss working with him on a daily basis, in some ways our relationship is better now that we've gotten the question of succession out of the way."[4]

Bill went on, "My wife and I had dinner with John and his wife recently, and I mentioned that I'd spent the day in a ten-hour management meeting. John just shook his head and laughed. That isn't the life for him."[5]

Many families decide to sell the family business at a certain point, or to fold it when the management reaches a certain age and wants to retire, not because they want to avoid tough family decisions, such as telling children they can't inherit the business leadership, but because it was the right time for the family and the business. In my experience, families who have accomplished this transition successfully not only prepare the business to be sold, but also prepare the family for the sale. The second type of planning typically involves, though is not limited to, preparing family members for change. What will happen professionally, post sale, for those members who worked in the business? How will those who own a percentage of the business handle a sudden increase of liquid wealth? This sort of preparation requires skills and practices that will be discussed later in this chapter.

A couple of years ago, I was asked to work with a family that decided to sell its business after two generations in existence. I was introduced to the patriarch, Ben, the son of the founder, who made the actual decision to sell with the counsel of his wife, Judith. Ben said to me, "I always saw the business as four walls that surrounded value, and it is time to cash in on that value." To their credit, Ben and Judith knew that the sale was more than selling assets. Their family, including numerous grandchildren, was close and they wanted to make sure the decision to sell had a positive impact on every member of it, even though they acknowledged that each was likely to experience the transition differently.

As part of my process, I spent time individually with each of the core family members: Ben, Judith, their four adult children, and their children's spouses. Three of the adult children were married with children of their own, and two had worked in the business most of their adult lives. In addition, the spouse of one of Ben and Judith's children worked in a leadership role in the business. No other family members were presently working in the family business. After these conversations, I met with Ben and Judith, and then, eventually, all the family members together, to share what I had learned and make suggestions for how to plan for the sale.

For this family, which had employed experts to help them focus on the sale of the business, the following topics would become part of planning the family for the sale.

- Raising the financial IQ and life IQ of the next generation, in anticipation of an increase in liquid wealth.
- Ben and Judith's children's focus on enhancing their parenting skills in the context of meaningful wealth for their children.
- The roles of different family members in Ben and Judith's family foundation.
- Career planning. Defining what type of work the three family members currently working in the family business wanted to do after the sale occurred. If they had the chance, would they want to work for the new owners? Or would they pursue other opportunities—and what kind?
- Understanding the process of change and transition, and how each family member was likely to experience it given their natural emotional and psychological "wiring."
- Clearly establishing shared values and purpose as a family.
- Identifying a new purpose or project that could continue to bring the family together—like the business had done—in addition to celebrating holidays and birthdays.

A year and a half after the sale, the family was doing great overall. They committed to an annual family meeting, and decided to leverage Ben and Judith's foundation as their new "family business" and a way to express their shared family value of giving and sharing with others. They continued to invest in raising their financial IQ and life IQ by working closely with their wealth manager, their tax and estate attorney, and me. As Ben and Judith had anticipated, everyone experienced the transition differently. This is normal. Some family members were initially sad that the business was no longer part of the family. Others felt a particular responsibility to help the long-term employees of the business manage the transition. The child who had worked in the business most of her adult life was still working on what she wanted to do next, professionally.

THE FAMILY BUSINESS AND OTHER SHARED FAMILY ASSETS

Last year, my wife and I decided to buy an iPod to be shared by our two youngest children. We knew the "sharing" part might not come easy, however we thought it would be a valuable contribution into their life IQs. This gift was one of their Christmas presents. They found the iPod wrapped with both their names on the tag, but even so my son took it and unwrapped it. "Awesome," he said, "thanks for getting *me* this." How quickly he forgot that his sister's name was also on the tag and that we'd said the gift was for both of them to share. Making an investment into our children's life IQs began early that Christmas morning.

All too often, the ability to share isn't the most natural thing to do. It requires intention, skill, and practice. What happened to our children and *their* shared iPod is a microcosm of what happens with many adults who have to share adult "toys" —things like businesses, homes, and inheritances in general—with their siblings and cousins. It's not that people don't want to share—although this is the case sometimes; it's more that sharing takes effort. Family members don't necessarily have the same perspectives, values, and interests. And if you add a little stress, lack of trust, or some conflict into the mix, sharing can be even harder.

There are numerous examples in my work of families that have to make a decision about a shared family asset. This could be a business, the use of a summer home, or the operation of a family foundation. Yes, even such a noble value as wanting to give to charity from a family foundation requires skills to decide which charity or charities to give to. I have witnessed families arguing because they disagree about their donations. "I would rather give to . . ." "That charity's mission also includes [*fill in the blank*] and I don't agree with that." "I believe we should only give to charities in our backyard."

It is easy to make a decision, if one person in the family (like the parent) funds the foundation and therefore makes the final decisions. All other family members follow along. However, when there is a decision to be made on a shared family asset by more than one person who has some skin in the game for the outcome of the decision, a decision requires intention and skill.

When I refer to a shared family asset, it does not necessarily mean that all family members technically own it or strategically direct it. However, it does mean this asset is part of the family portfolio of capitals and therefore plays a role in the family system—as distant or close as it may be from family members. In many cases, the family's shared asset, such as a business, is like another child in the family: significant time, emotion, and treasure have been invested into it. In some cases, even more has been invested in it than in some of the actual children in the family. Another shared asset could be a home that has been in the family for a couple of generations and has deep emotional significance to some family members while others perceive it as just another house in the family.

In my experience of working with multiple generations of a family that has a shared asset, the elder generation tends to make the final decision or steps in when they sense members of the younger generation are beginning to have conflict. This is the same as my wife or me stepping in when our two children disagree over whose turn is it to play with the iPod.

Because each family inevitably has a shared family asset, however small or large it may be, it is important that a family develop the skills to collaborate and make decisions together. To assist them in developing these skills, I will often have my clients go through a governance exercise.

It typically goes like this: I will identify a shared family asset that has relevance to most, if not all, of the adult family members—let's say a ski house in Aspen. I will ask the elder generation not to participate in the initial part of the exercise. I will then pose the following scenario to the next generation: "Your parents have asked you to make the following decision regarding the sale of the family's ski house in Aspen. Someone has made an offer 15 percent above market rates to buy the ski home and they want a response in the next fifteen days or they will withdraw their offer. Your parents want you to make the decision without them."

I then add, "For the purpose of this exercise, I do not want you to make the actual decision, I would like you to propose a process for how you all will make the decision together in the next fifteen days." After this setup, I divide them into groups to work on their proposed decision-making processes.

After a while, I ask each group to share their proposed process with one another as well as their parents. I ask the parents just to listen to their children's proposals and not to weigh in. The last part of the governance exercise is for the entire family to work together to integrate the best of each of the proposals into one governance process for the family to be used in the future to manage real-life cases like the hypothetical one I gave them. This is a very powerful first-time experience for most families, especially those in the next generation, and these skills are vital to their long-term success and planning how to manage their shared family assets.

Similar to Ben and Judith, who knew the sale of their business involved more than planning for the sale of its assets, whether we are planning to run a business together or to share a family asset, such as a car, home, vineyard, plane, family bank, foundation, and yes, even something as small as an iPod, the hidden key is that it isn't only about planning for the financial asset, but also about planning for the human assets: the "business" of the family and our intended legacy.

As reflected throughout this book, when we prepare for a family "trip," like working in business together or sharing another type of family asset, relying on our spiritual capital to act as our GPS system is fundamental to the process. Our spiritual capital will ground the process in the core values and purpose of its members, and allow for God, the Divine, or transcendent wisdom to provide the perspective not found in our paper maps.

In addition, knowledge and skills are required for these types of trips, which I will now describe.

FAMILY SYSTEMS AND FAMILY COMPETENCE

Before describing the skills required to successfully navigate a family's trip, like working in a family business, it is important to have an understanding of systems. I have found a systems framework and its related concepts invaluable to me and for the client families I serve. In some cases, it has been the key to unlocking the potential in my client's lives.

A family is a social system, made up of members who interact and are interdependent with the other members. A mobile suspended above an infant's crib has been used as a metaphor for the interactions that happen among family members: If you move one part of a mobile it has a ripple effect throughout the entire mobile system. This metaphor is vital to remember when making important decisions, such as transferring wealth or selling a family business, because of the implications for those directly impacted by the decision and those who may be impacted a generation later. I not only spend time with my clients helping them think through the intended consequences of their family wealth decisions, but also the unintended consequences. For example, when Ben made his decision to sell the family business, he and Judith answered, "What may be the impact on the adult children who work in the family business most of their adult lives if the family business is sold?" Understanding that answer was part of the work we did together.

Unlike mobiles, family systems are emotional and existential rather than kinetic systems. They are emotional systems in that their members share a pattern of behaviors that guide their interactions, emotional responses, and attitudes. They are existential systems because there is an unconscious, and sometimes conscious search for meaning within the family. People naturally ask, "Who am I?" in the context of their families, as well as asking, "Who am I?" in the context of God or the universe. Running a family business successfully and making big decisions within the context of a family business requires us to understand that there is a sophisticated integration of the business system and the family system. What happens inside one of these systems may have an unintended ripple effect on the other. Rest assured, whether or not a family plans accordingly these systems will have ripple effects on each other.

Understanding that a family is an emotional system would

seem like common sense. However, it is important to note that an emotional system is not just referring to feelings such as sadness, anger, or happiness. A systems definition of an emotional system incorporates the needs of members for things such as food, shelter, safety, love, mating, and nurturing of the young. This is important, because we too often mistakenly focus on overt feelings, such as anger, when we're communicating with one another instead of trying to understand the other person's need or his or her *why* for thinking and behaving as he or she does. Understanding the need motivating another person completely transforms how to manage differences or problem solve.

It is also important to understand that a family is also an *existential* system—meaning, a source of meaning. It helps people define themselves when they do it in the context of their families. This explains the important dynamic between family members' dependence on, and independence from one another. In systems theory nomenclature, people seek to create a psychological balance between being autonomous and remaining intimately connected to their families of origin. This understanding is particularly vital to establishing healthy parent-child and sibling relationships.

Regarding the parent-child relationship, the separation or individuation process that is necessary as a child matures may be interpreted, especially during the teenage years when the separation is being initiated, as the belief, "My child is a rebel" or "My child is not following my rules." Sometimes, parents who establish a business may wonder why none of their children want to come into it and work alongside them. Yes, it is true that sometimes a business is not aligned with a child's skills or interests. Additionally, many children, unconsciously and consciously, want to set their own courses and not live in the shadow of their parents—or grandparents, or great-grandparents for that matter.

Regarding the sibling relationship, in the spirit of being individuals, some define themselves by *not* being what a brother or sister is. In the case of a family business, a younger sibling may not want to report to an older sibling with a higher status in a family business. From their perspective, this would only perpetuate the nature of the relationship growing up. Interestingly, this type of avoidance is rarely a conscious process, and it doesn't explain or predict every potential scenario. Keep in mind, however, that it could provide deep insight into the planning of your family's success as well as the success of your family business.

Given that life, especially the life of a family that co-owns or co-manages a business, will provide its inevitable transitions, challenges, and blessings, it is vitally important to develop the skills and practices needed to face what life offers. Based on decades of research with couples and families, Robert Beavers and Robert Hampson created a theory of *family competence,* which is defined as the family's ability to perform the "necessary tasks of organizing and managing itself."[6] Family competence measures the ability (or lack of ability) to communicate, coordinate, negotiate, establish clear roles and goals, problem solve, adapt to new situations, manage conflict, accept responsibility, be autonomous, and have confidence in itself.[7] This model is based less on *homeostasis*—attempting to maintain the status quo is viewed by experts as a characteristic of less healthy family systems—and more on the concept of *morphogenesis,* or a spontaneous, flexible structure that's open to growth and change and is responsive to new stimulation. Members of healthy families, those that function at a high level of competence, demonstrate a capacity, among other things, to organize themselves, receive input from each other, negotiate differences, quickly resolve conflicts, and communicate openly. In my experience, all these skills are vital to the long-term success of a family.

THE BUSINESS OF THE FAMILY

There are many resources available to help individuals and families plan for the success of their family businesses or to help them manage their other financial assets. In addition, various practices have been written about that contribute to the success of a family. Writing a multigenerational family vision, mission, and shared values statement is just one example. Here, we will focus on skills that are more rarely addressed, yet which are foundational to the success of the *business of the family.* They enable everything else to happen successfully across the generations, irrespective of which family assets might exist. In addition, the skills that will be described enable a family to successfully create a shared family vision or mission statement, for example.

The fifteen foundational relationship skills of successful families include:

1. Communicating: Family members are able to clearly articulate what they feel, think, and need, and to use language reflecting "ownership" of their feelings, thoughts, and needs. They use "I" statements when communicating.

2. Listening: Family members are not only able to hear the words of the others, but also to understand those words by reflecting back what they've heard. While listening, they intentionally try to put themselves in the shoes of the speaker to better understand what they are hearing. It has been said that we have two ears and one mouth, so we should listen twice as much as we speak.

3. Staying open: Family members acknowledge that they may not know everything there is to know about a topic, situation, or person. They maintain a posture of being receptive to new information by asking discovery questions and by not discarding information that doesn't fit their preexisting assumptions.

4. Adapting: Family members find ways to adapt to new information, circumstances, and people. They demonstrate the willingness to learn and grow.

5. Negotiating: Family members are clear on what is negotiable and not negotiable for them as individuals, and in situations where negotiation within the family will serve a higher goal or purpose. The members do not see negotiation as a win-lose proposition. In my experience, the sign of a good negotiation is that each party should walk away feeling they got something they wanted from the negotiation.

6. Managing differences: Family members understand that not everyone in the family will have the same exact perspectives, values, or interests, and so strive to find the commonality between them and to build bridges that will connect them without sacrificing their perspectives, values, and interests. In addition, family members see their differences as a way to expand their perspectives and possibly identify new solutions.

7. Defining roles: Family members understand that in addition to the many roles they play (spouse, significant other, grandparent, parent, child, sibling, and so forth) they are also stakeholders in the family. This understanding allows each of them to connect to a higher purpose: the success of the family. In other words, each has a responsibility to contribute.

If there is a family business, it is important to be clear on what role, if any, each family member has in the family business (for example, is this person an owner, an employee, a manager, or a board member). During group interactions or conversations between two family members, it is important to be clear on which "hat" each is supposed to "be wearing." At a given moment, is it a father talking to a son or a boss talking to an employee?

8. Goal setting: Family members know how to set short and long-term goals, whether these goals pertain to their own development, or the development of others and a business. As importantly, family members know the difference between setting process goals versus setting outcome goals. The former are defined and measurable activities that are intended to contribute to achieving the latter.

9. Decision making: Family members have the understanding of various structures of governance of the family business (for example, an assembly, a committee, a counsel, a constitution, a board of directors, an advisory group) and decision-making strategies (for example, autocratic, simple and super majorities, consensus, unanimous, cumulative voting). With this knowledge, each understands that the ability to make a decision together is the primary goal; the structure and strategy is then applied to fit each respective decision.

10. Not assuming: Family members should not assume they know the motivations and intentions of the others. Instead, if there is a question about why another did, said, or felt something, or a sense that something was not clearly understood, one family member would go directly to another family member to ask questions and arrive at an accurate understanding.

11. Accepting personal responsibility: Family members understand that although they are interacting at times within the context of the family—and as a result, can be affected by other's actions, decisions, or words—each is ultimately responsible for how he or she responds, interprets, and assimilates the actions, decisions, and words of others into his or her own life. Similarly, each person is ultimately responsible for the actions, decisions, or words he or she takes, makes, and says, or doesn't take, make, or say.

12. Pursuing happiness: Family members understand that there are things they can do to contribute to their own lasting happiness, and to the lasting happiness of other family members: for example, expressing gratitude, finding a purpose, and giving and sharing.

13. Forgiving: Family members understand that it is possible for one family member to disappoint, hurt, or outright abuse another, unintentionally or otherwise, and that it is important in such cases for the injured party to work though his or her process of forgiving. Forgiveness may possibly help heal a troubled relationship—depending on the severity of the offense. At a minimum, it will help the aggrieved family member heal and move on.

14. Handling transitions: Even though knowing the process of change or transition is not necessarily a skill, I want to add this to the foundational skills list, as change is inevitable. Whether a change involves going from a single to a married status, having a child, undergoing a divorce, losing someone we deeply loved, inheriting wealth, achieving an important goal, or selling a business, it is helpful for family members to understand that not all of them will experience the change or transition the same way, and on the same timetable.

15. Trusting: The level of trust one family member has toward another depends on how high the level of the aforementioned skills are within a family. For example, if a family member is not a good listener, is not interested in negotiating, is ineffective in managing differences, and doesn't take personal responsibility for his or her actions, there will tend to be a low level of trust when interacting with this person. Trusting another is a deeply personal decision. Some family members start by fully trusting their families just because they're family, and others start from a posture that their family members have to prove themselves and earn their trust. In either case, the ability to trust those who are trustworthy is very important to the success of a family.

THE ALPHA AND OMEGA

I used to lead a team of professionals that focused on building work teams around the globe. After many years of experience building thousands of teams (as well as taking some teams apart), we developed the following expression: "We could ensure a successful work team if we could just remove the people from the equation." The same is true with families. It is the family that we start and end with. The people in the family are our X factor for its success. It is the business of the family that we have to intentionally plan for, and this planning is both a science and an art.

The list of skills in the preceding section is an aspirational list. I don't know a family that has mastered each and every one of them. However, those who continue to enhance their skills in the aforementioned areas increase the odds of having success when interacting across the generations, whether in managing the business of the family or a family business.

So whether you are planning for a wealth transfer, doing some next-generation preparation, giving and sharing your capitals, working together in business, or making a decision about any other type of family asset, the hidden secret is to ensure you plan for the business of the family. How you plan and the skills you demonstrate today and tomorrow will have a direct impact on your present and future legacy.

Given this, take a few moments to assess your skills and those of your family using the following table where "never" scores a 1, "rarely" scores a 2, "sometimes" scores a 3, "often" scores a 4, and "always" scores a 5. Remember, if you find you are less competent than you would like to be with a particular skill, you can choose to work on it. Circle your answers.

COMMUNICATING

1   2   3   4   5

LISTENING

1   2   3   4   5

STAYING OPEN

1   2   3   4   5

ADAPTING

1   2   3   4   5

NEGOTIATING

1   2   3   4   5

MANAGING DIFFERENCES

1   2   3   4   5

DEFINING ROLES

1   2   3   4   5

GOAL SETTING

1   2   3   4   5

DECISION MAKING

1   2   3   4   5

NOT ASSUMING

1   2   3   4   5

ACCEPTING RESPONSIBILITY

1   2   3   4   5

PURSUING HAPPINESS

1   2   3   4   5

FORGIVING

1   2   3   4   5

HANDLING TRANSITIONS

1   2   3   4   5

TRUSTING

1   2   3   4   5

FINAL THOUGHTS

Do not forsake wisdom, and she will protect you;
Love her, and she will watch over you.
The beginning of wisdom is this: Get wisdom.
Though it cost all you have, get understanding.
Cherish her, and she will exalt you;
Embrace her, and she will honor you.
—Proverbs (4:6–8)

I trust that as a result of reading this book, your legacy journey will no longer be a road less traveled. I hope you've been ignited with greater intention and inspiration. Now that you've begun to secure your *whys, whats,* and *hows,* a clearer path toward finding your answers to the five most important family wealth decisions impacting your living and lasting legacy lies before you.

No longer will you be misinformed about how to plan for your family's legacy. No longer will you limit yourself to the one-dimensional conventional wisdom masked in "paper maps."

Remember, your spiritual capital is the most important capital you have to help you navigate both your important family wealth decisions, and the other important life decisions you'll inevitably have to make.

I pray for God's speed to be with you as you live your legacy each day and make a positive imprint on your community, the world, and your family for generations to come.

If you would like to share how this book has positively impacted your family's legacy, please email your story to LegacyStories@LegacyCapitals.com. Please note in your email if it is okay to share your stories with others. If it is, it will allow your legacy to bless and inspire others.

ACKNOWLEDGMENTS

M any individuals and organizations have contributed to who I am and what I've learned over the past quarter of a century. As a result, in some indirect way they have contributed to this book. The following list is an attempt to acknowledge some of them.

To my wife, Kristin, I could not have accomplished this without you; nor would I have wanted to. Your love, patience, challenge, wisdom, and intelligence can be found throughout the fabric of this book. More specifically, thank you for your willingness and endurance, listening to me at all hours of the day and night talking about my ideas for the book. You are not only an amazing wife and mother, you are also my best friend. Thank you, baby! To my children, thank you. You are my inspiration and I hope to help you live *your* legacy.

To my parents, what can I say? In addition to God, you are the reason why I am here. I love you deeply and let this book reflect positively in your legacy. To my brother, Robert, and sister, Roslyn, and their families, thank you. We have shared such an intimate legacy together and may we continue to live the legacy we desire. I want to thank the many generations of the Coppola and Orlando families: grandparents, aunts, uncles, cousins, nieces, and nephews. Our family has taught me so much about being part of a multigenerational family. Thank you to my mother-in-law and father-in-law for the love and support you have provided to me.

To my dear friends David Biedel, Valerie Charles, Marlon DeBlasio, Yniol DelPino, Chris Firestone, John Hoyne, Diane Prete, Chad and Danielle Reyes, Barbara Rotunda, and Linda Tucker, thank you. We have shared so much together and I look forward to our continued relationships.

I want to thank all the individuals and families who have hired me to serve them, and in turn, taught me so much. In spirit, you all are the coauthors of this book.

There are many relationships that are dear to me that started as professional, and have grown to be personal and a blessing to my life. Thank you, David Karp, Paul Pagnato, and team; Augie Cenname, Michael Denti, Charles Jarrett, Larry Manierre, Peter Motta, Audrey Tuckerman, Steve Vuyevich, and team; Frank Migliazzo, Frank Morelli, and team; Nadia Allaudin; Devon Baranski; Chip Conley; Jennifer Povlitz; Greg Sarian; Linda Stirling; Mark Brookfield, Jeff Erdmann, Robert Giannetti, and team.

There are many others who paved the way, gave me opportunities to learn and grow, and/or added value to my life. To name just a few, thank you: Deborah Aldredge, Stacy Allred, Fredda Herz Brown, Robert Calabrese, Mollie Colavita, Charles Collier, Stephanie Constantino, Riley Etheridge, Lee Hausner, Bill Hodges, Jay Hughes, Dennis Jaffe, Greg McGauley, Theodore Malloch, Michael Papedis, Michael Parker, Nancy Petrucelli, Austin Philbin, Martin Seligman, Scott Shaw, Phil Sieg, John Thiel, Kevin Wallace, John A. Warnick, Steve Weiner, Elliot Weissbluth, Peter White, and Kathy Wiseman.

A special thank you to all those who took the time out of their busy schedules to read the book manuscript and provide a written endorsement.

Thank you to Covenant Church, the Doylestown Kingdom Advisor Study Group, Doylestown Library, the Purposeful Planning Institute, the Practice Management Consulting Group at Merrill Lynch, and the Family Firm Institute.

The creation of this book would have literally not been possible without Lincoln Square Books. In particular, Stephanie Gunning, cofounder and senior partner, and Peter Rubie. Stephanie, you are amazing. Only you know the details of the evolution of this book and your wise guidance is deeply appreciated and valued. May your hard work be rewarded by now seeing this book help others live their legacy and leave a positive imprint on their families, community, and the world.

Thanks to Jennifer Prost of Jennifer Prost Public Relations for her partnership in launching this book.

To my Heavenly Father through His son, Jesus Christ, thank you for a deeply blessed life filled with challenge, purpose, and true wealth. I also want to acknowledge the many other spiritual leaders who remind us that we are not only material beings, but also spiritual beings, and there is more to this world than what we can see with our eyes and touch with our hands.

NOTES

INTRODUCTION

1. Regina Herzlinger, contributor, "The Legacy of Steve Jobs" *Working Knowledge* (Harvard Business School, October 7, 2011). Website: http://hbswk.hbs.edu/item/6848.html.
2. Friedrich Nietzsche, as quoted by Viktor E. Frankl in Man's *Search for Meaning* (Boston, MA.: Beacon Press, 2006): p. 76. The original text comes from Nietzsche's book *Twilight of the Idols, or, How to Philosophize with a Hammer* (in German: *Götzen-Dämmerung, oder, Wie man mit dem Hammer philoso-phiert*), which was published in 1889.

PART ONE: THE ROAD LESS TRAVELED

Epigraph. M. Scott Peck, *The Road Less Traveled* (New York: Touchstone, 2003): p. 83.

CHAPTER 1: NAVIGATING YOUR LEGACY

Epigraph. Pierre Teilhard de Chardin, *The Phenomenon of Man* (1955).

1. Source: A flyer from Infiniti.
2. InvestorWords.com defines *black swan* as: "Colloquial term for any

extremely rare event. The term was popularized by a book by Nassim Nicholas Taleb, entitled *The Black Swan*, and was based on a previous belief (now a misconception) that all swans were white and that black swans did not exist. The term is frequently used in the finance and investing sectors to denote an event that is unexpected, and impossible to accurately predict."

3. Craig Hamilton, "Excellence Is Not Enough: An Interview with Anthony Robbins" (accessed August 21, 2013) New York Power Team website: http://newyorkpowerteam.com/articles.

4. Blaise Pascal, *Pensées,* 1670. Source: Gutenberg.org.

5. ThinkExist.com.

6. Martin E.P. Seligman and his colleagues conducted this type of research, which is referenced in his book *Authentic Happiness* (New York: Free Press, 2003).

7. The Gallup Organization, "The Spiritual State of the Union: The Role of Spiritual Commitment in the United States" (Princeton, N.J., 2006).

8. George Gallup, III, and Theodore Roosevelt Malloch, "The Spiritual State of the Union: The Role of Spiritual Commitment in the United States: Additional Observations for Purposes of Discussion." (Princeton, N.J.: The Gallup Organization, 2006): p. 3.

9. Eric Weiner, "Americans: Undecided about God?" *New York Times* (December 10, 2011): p. SR5.

10. James Atlas, "Buddhists' Delight," *New York Times* (June 17, 2012): p. SR4.

11. James E. Hughes, Jr., *Family Wealth—Keeping It in the Family* (New York: Bloomberg Press, 2004): p. xv.

12. Deepak Chopra, *The Third Jesus* (Three Rivers Press, 2009): p. 54.

13. On Thursday, April 10, 2008, Paul Schervish, Ph.D., Director of Boston College's Center for Wealth and Philanthropy, presented the fifth annual Thomas H. Lake Lecture on Faith and Giving at the Center on Philanthropy at Indiana University. His lecture was entitled "Receiving and Giving as Spiritual Exercise."

14. The book my clients referenced was Jim Collins, *Built to Last: Successful Habits of Visionary Companies* (New York: HarperBusiness, 2004).

15. Simon Sinek, "How Great Leaders Inspire Action," filmed September 2009 at TedxPuget Sound (posted May 2010). Website: TED.com.

16. Michael E. Gerber, *The E-Myth Revisited* (New York: HarperCollins, 1995): pp. 206–7.

17. Ibid: p. 256.

CHAPTER 2: PREPARING FOR YOUR LEGACY JOURNEY

Epigraph. Sir George Pickering. According to Charles Garfield, *Peak Performers* (New York: William Morrow, 1986): p. 156. Albert Einstein had this quote chalked on the blackboard in his office at Princeton University.

1. Quotationsbook.com.

2. Theodore Roosevelt Malloch, *Spiritual Enterprise* (Encounter Books, 2008): p. 119.

3. Naturalist Charles Darwin is often misquoted as saying that it is not the smartest or the strongest of a species that survives, but the most adaptable, or "fittest." He never used these exact words. However, in *On the Origin of Species* (1859), a seminal book whose title was shortened to *The Origin of Species* in 1872, he did coin the term *natural selection*. In this work he presented evidence that diverse life descended from a common ancestry over the course of generations, through a

branching pattern of evolution. He posited that the struggle for survival in the wild leads to changes in species similar to changes produced by artificial selection processes used in controlled breeding.

4. Friedrich Nietzsche, as quoted by Viktor E. Frankl in *Man's Search for Meaning* (Boston, MA.: Beacon Press, 2006): p. 76.

PART TWO: LANDMARKS ON YOUR FAMILY WEALTH JOURNEY

Epigraph: Tavis Smiley. I found this quote on Goodreads.com, on a page devoted to the topic of legacy.

CHAPTER 3: THE PURSUIT OF HAPPINESS

Epigraph. The author of this quote is unknown to me.

1. Aristotle, *Nichomachean Ethics,* Book 1, Section 7, written 350 B.C.E., translated by W.D. Ross. Website: http://classics.mit.edu/Aristotle/nicomachaen.1.i.html.

2. James Hughes, *Family Wealth—Keeping It in the Family* (New York: Bloomberg Press, 2004): p. 43.

3. About Buddha website: http://www.aboutbuddha.net/buddha_quotes_on_money _and_wealth.html.

4. Martin E.P. Seligman, *Authentic Happiness* (New York: Free Press, 2003), p. 55.

5. Graeme Wood, "Secret Fears of the Super-Rich," *Atlantic* (February 24, 2011). Website: http://theatlantic.com.

6. Ibid.

7. Ecclesiastes (2: 3–11), *The Holy Bible, New International Version* (Biblica, Inc, 2011). Website: http://www.biblegateway.com/versions/ New-International-Version-NIV-Bible.

8. Martin E.P. Seligman, in a lecture, "The New Era of Positive

Psychology" videotaped at TED2004 in February 2004.
Website:
http://www.ted.com/talks/martin_seligman_on_the_state_of
_psychology.html.

9. Martin E.P. Seligman, *Flourish* (Free Press, 2011).

10. Seligman, *Authentic Happiness*: p. 60.

11. Michael I. Norton, in a lecture, "How to Buy Happiness" videotaped at TEDxCambridge in November 2011. Website: http://www.ted.com/talks/michael_norton_how_to_buy _happiness.html.

12. Barbara Walters, "Billionaire Secrets: What They Know That Can Change Your Life," *20/20* (aired October 28, 2011). Website: ABC.com.

13. Clayton M. Christensen, *How Will You Measure Your Life?* (New York: HarperBusiness, 2012): p. 6.

14. Clayton M. Christensen, "How Will You Measure Your Life?" *Harvard Business Review* (July 2010). Website: http://hbr.org/2010/07/how-will-you-measure-your-life/ ar/1.

15. Ibid.

16. Randy Pausch, *The Last Lecture* (New York: Hyperion, 2008): p. 197–198.

17. The Ethical Will of Frank Perdue. Website: http://www.signallake.com/innovation/THE_ETHICAL _WILL_Frank_Perdue.pdf.

18. BrainyQuote.com.

CHAPTER 4: TRANSFERRING YOUR WEALTH

Epigraph. Cited in an article by Tim Voorhees, "Why Most Families Lose Their Wealth by the Third Generation," *Wealth Counsel Quarterly* (April 2009). Website: https://www.wealthcounsel.com/newsletter/TimVoorhees

-WhyMostFamiliesLoseTheirWealthbytheThirdGeneration.pdf.
1. George Stalk and Henry Foley, "Avoid the Traps That Can Destroy Family Businesses," *Harvard Business Review* (January-February 2012). Website: http://hbr.org/2012/01/avoid-the-traps-that-can -destroy-family-businesses/ar/1.
2. Roy D. Williams, *For Love and Money: A Comprehensive Guide to the Successful Generational Transfer of Wealth, Institute for Preparing Heirs* (1997). A study of 3,250 families.
3. Plato, *Apology*, 38a. This remark comes from a speech made by Socrates in 399 B.C.E. to the men of Athens after being condemned to death. Website: http://www.perseus.tufts.edu/hopper/text?doc=plat.%20 apol.%2038a.
4. *Born Rich,* a documentary film directed by Jamie Johnson (2003).

CHAPTER 5: NEXT-GENERATION PREPARATION

Epigraphs. George Bernard Shaw (1856–1950), British playwright and critic, said this during aspeech at the Municipal Technical College and School of Art in Brighton, England in 1907. Elisabeth Kübler-Ross. Elisabeth Kübler-Ross Foundation website: http://www.ekrfoundation.org/quotes.
1. PNC Wealth Management, "Wealth and Values Survey: Millionaires and Legacy" (January 2013).
2. *U.S. Trust Insights on Wealth and Worth 2012.* Website: http://www.ustrust.com/ust/pages/Insights-on-Wealth-and -Worth.aspx.
3. John Stovall, *The Ultimate Gift* (Colorado Springs, CO.: David C. Cook, 2001).
4. Quoto.com.

CHAPTER 6: GIVING AND SHARING

Epigraph. Mother Teresa. Website: ThinkExist.com.

1. The Giving Pledge mission statement reads: "The Giving Pledge is a commitment by the world's wealthiest individuals and families to dedicate the majority of their wealth to philanthropy." You can read profiles of the growing number of billionaires who have made this pledge on the official website: http://givingpledge.org.

2. Bill Gates. Source: http://www.nptrust.org/history-of-giving/philanthropic-quotes.

3. "The New Philanthropists: More Sophisticated, More Demanding—and Younger," *Knowledge@Wharton* (April 24, 2013).Website: http://knowledge.wharton.upenn.edu/article.cfm?articleid=3234.

4. Victor Hugo, *Les Miserables* (1862).

5. Michael I. Norton, in a lecture, "How to Buy Happiness" videotaped at TEDxCambridge in November 2011. Website: http://www.ted.com/talks/michael_norton_how_to_buy_happiness.html.

6. John C. Maxwell, speaking at the 2013 Chick-fil-A Leadercast (aired May 10, 2013).

7. Hannah Shaw Grove, John Morris, Richard Orlando, "Purposeful Travel." Website: http://legacycapitals.com/resources.

8. *Knowledge@Wharton.*

9. I saw Caine's video during the 2013 Chick-fil-A Leadercast teleconference, and subsequently searched "Caine's Arcade" on Wikipedia and found more details: http://en.wikipedia.org/wiki/Caine%27s_Arcade.

CHAPTER 7: TAKING CARE OF THE BUSINESS OF THE FAMILY

Epigraph. Anthony Brandt. Website: Goodreads.com.

1. Grant Gordon and Nigel Nicholson, *Family Wars* (London, U.K.: Kogan Page, 2010).
2. John A. Davis, speaking at the Family Firm Institute Conference in Boston, MA. in October 2011.
3. Family Business Institute website: http://www.familybusinessinstitute.com/index.php/Succession-Planning.
4. Bill Marriott, "Marriott's Executive Chairman on Choosing the First Nonfamily CEO," *Harvard Business Review* (May 2013). Website: http://hbr.org/2013/05/marriotts-executive-chairman-on-choosing-the-first-nonfamily-ceo/ar/1.
5. Ibid.
6. W. Robert Beavers and Robert B. Hampson, "Measuring Family Competence: The Beavers Systems Model," in Froma Walsh, editor, *Normal Family Processes* (New York: The Guilford Press, 1993): pp. 73–103.
7. Ibid.

FINAL THOUGHTS

Epigraph. Proverbs (4: 6–8), *The Holy Bible, New International Version* (Biblica, Inc, 2011). Website: http://www.biblegateway.com/versions/New-International-Version-NIV-Bible.

RESOURCES

If you are interested in learning more about the topics in this book, please go to LegacyCapitals.com. The resources you'll find on our company website include:

- *Solutions for individuals and families,* such as: multigenerational family meetings, next-generation workshops, couples workshops, and individual coaching.
- *Solutions for advisors,* such as: advisor workshops, and individual and team coaching.
- *Resources:* our blog, articles, videos, and the latest news.
- *Store:* print materials, digital classes, and other tools.
- *Media kit:* a bio, photo, and fact sheet for speaking engagements and other venues, and press releases.
- *Links to follow us* on: Twitter, Facebook, LinkedIn, and YouTube.

There are many other resources to be referenced, and I would like to highlight just a handful of them. If you are interested in a particular resource not listed on this page, feel free to contact me via LegacyCapitals.com and I will try to point you in the right direction.

BOOKS

James Hughes, *Family Wealth—Keeping It in the Family.* New York: Bloomberg Press, 2004.

Martin E.P. Seligman, *Authentic Happiness.* New York: Free Press, 2003.

John Stovall, *The Ultimate Gift.* Colorado Springs, CO.: David C. Cook, 2001.

ORGANIZATIONS

Family Firm Institute:
www.FFI.org

Legacy Capitals Forum group found on:
www.LinkedIn.com/groups

Purposeful Planning Institute:
http://PurposefulPlanninginstitute.com

Technology, Entertainment, Design (TED):
www.TED.com

ABOUT THE AUTHOR

For the past quarter century, **Richard Orlando, Ph.D.,** founder and CEO of Legacy Capitals LLC, has worked globally with individuals, such as executives, entrepreneurs, professional athletes, and entertainers, as well as families, work teams, and organizations, who strive for success or have already reached significant levels of success.

More specifically, Dr. Orlando serves as a trusted advisor, consultant, and coach to some of the world's wealthiest families—some of which lead very successful family businesses. In addition, he has worked with *Barron's* Top 100 Financial Advisors, as well as leaders and high-performing teams nationally and internationally.

Dr. Orlando has an interdisciplinary background, holding degrees in computer science, business, and psychology. After earning a Bachelor of Science degree in computer science and business from St. John's University, he pursued a career on Wall Street and earned his Series 7 and 63 licenses. Returning to school, he received a master's degree in counseling/theology from Trinity International University. Continuing his education, he earned a doctorate in family systems from Seton Hall University, during which time he interned with the New York Giants football team. His dissertation research focused on wealth management family teams. Dr. Orlando also earned a certificate in family wealth advising from the Family Firm Institute and holds a certified professional coach designation from an International Coach Federation accredited program.

Dr. Orlando has been featured in numerous publications such as the *New York Times, Wall Street Journal online, Private Wealth Magazine, CFA Magazine, Merrill Lynch Advisor, Research, Bloomberg Wealth Manager, On Wall Street,* and *Registered Rep.* He has conducted hundreds of presentations to various groups and organizations, among them Merrill Lynch, U.S. Trust, High-Tower, Dynasty Financial Partners, Janney Montgomery Scott, Young Presidents Organization, and Vistage International. He's also spoken at the conferences of Barron's, Securities Industry Institute, and Investment Management Consultants Association.

Dr. Orlando is on the board of director's of Urban Hope in Staten Island, New York. He was born and raised in New York City, and currently resides in Bucks County, Pennsylvania, with his wife and their children.

INDEX

A

accomplishment, 62
adaptation, 119, 160–161
advisors. *See* professional advisors
affluenza, 58, 60–61, 115, 118, 122
agape, 129–130, 140
age, planning considerations, 100–102, 108
"Americans: Undecided about God?" (Weiner), 25–26
assets, 19, 44–45, 72, 89–92, 119, 153–156
assumptions, avoiding, 162
Atlas, James, 26
Authentic Happiness (Seligman), 58
autonomy, 156–158

B

Barone Ricasoli Winery, 150
Beavers, Robert, 159
beliefs, inventory of, 83–85
"Billionaire Secrets" (20/20 episode), 64
black swans, 19, 157
Born Rich (documentary), 83–84
"Buddhists' Delight" (Atlas), 26
budgets, 115
Built to Last (Collins), 31

C

Caine's Arcade (documentary), 142
capitals. *See also* spiritual capital
    financial, 5, 40, 41, 46, 50, 57–58
    human, 43, 47, 50
    intellectual, 41–42, 47, 50
    social, 42–43, 44, 47, 50
    type overview, 5
challenges, 63, 99–100
change, inevitability of, 163
character, judging, 118–119
children. *See* next generation
Chopra, Deepak, 28
Christensen, Clayton M., 65
chronology, planning considerations, 100–102, 108
coaches/coaching, 113–114, 138–139
Collins, Jim, 31
communication
    about money, 115, 122–123
    of beliefs, 83–85
    in business of family, 160
    of expectations, 122–123
    in generational transfer, 91–92, 122–125
    lack of, 72–73
    pitfalls of, 101
    storytelling, 114
compassion, 130
competence, judging, 118–119
connection, vs. autonomy, 158
consequences, 134, 157
control, 19, 89–92
core virtues, 24

D

Davis, John A., 149
decision making
    by families, 162
    in family businesses, 147–148, 154, 156–158
    governance exercise, 155–156
    spirituality role, 20–23, 74–75
differences, managing, 161

E

emotional intelligence, 120
emotional responses, 120, 157–158
The E-Myth Revisited (Gerber), 32–33
entitlement mentality, 61, 83
equal, vs. fair, 88, 91–92
equation, for spiritual capital, 27
estate planning, 6, 20–21, 68, 75, 87–88, 94
ethical wills, 67
existential systems, 157–158
expectations, 104–106, 120, 122–124
expertise, giving role, 137
external forces, 120

F

fair, vs. equal, 88, 91–92
faith, 5, 19, 22–23, 27–28, 80, 81–82. *See also* spirituality
families
    happiness as purpose of, 55
    preparation of, vs. asset preparation, 19, 72
    relationship skills for, 160–163
family businesses
    vs. business of family, 160–163
    decision making in, 147–148, 154, 156–158
    interpersonal dynamics in, 148–153
    sale of, 151–152
    as shared assets, 153–156

systemic framework for, 156–159
family competence, 159
family governance, 148
Family Wars (Gordon and Nicholson), 147
Family Wealth (Hughes), 26, 55
fear
of asset loss, 7
regarding wealth transfer, 58–59, 110, 116, 122
financial capital, 5, 40, 41, 46, 50, 57–58
financial giving, 137–138
financial IQ, 99, 106–112
financial issues, list of, 19
first-generational mindset, 117
FISHS framework, 40–50, 99, 136–140
Flourish (Seligman), 62
forgiveness, 163

G

Gates, Bill, 127–128
generational transfer. *See also* next-generation preparation
belief inventory, 83–85
case history, 78–80
communication about, 122–123
failure of, 72–73
giving vs. wealth transfer, 89–92
overview of, 95
planning for, 74
role of faith in, 81–82
timing of, 93–94
values/purpose determination, 76–82
what vs. how much structure, 83–88
generations, definitions of, 100–103
generosity, 130
Gerber, Michael, 32–33
giving. *See also* sharing
children and, 114, 120
consequences of, 134

happiness role, 63
vs. philanthropy, 129
process of, 131–134
of time/talent, 134–136
vs. transfer of wealth, 89–92
while alive, 143
Giving Pledge, 127
goal setting, 161–162
golden rule, 112–113, 133–134
Gordon, Grant, 147
governance exercise, 155–156
GPS analogy, for legacy planning, 16–18
gratitude, 61, 63
Grove, Hannah Shaw, 136

H

Hampson, Robert, 159
happiness
    attributes of, 62–64, 68–70
    of children, 116–117
    money and, 56–61, 67–68
    of parents, 112
    positive psychology and, 62–64
    purpose and, 65–68
    pursuit of, 55, 120, 162–163
hedonic treadmill, 60–61
Herzlinger, Regina, 2–3
homeostasis, 159
hope, for the future, 63
horizontal dimensions, of generational transfer, 88
"How Great Leaders Inspire Action" (Sinek), 32
"How Will You Measure Your Life?" (Christensen), 65
Hughes, James F., Jr., 26, 55
Hugo, Victor, 130
human assets, planning and, 156
human capital, 43, 47, 50
human giving, 139–140

I

improbable events, 19, 157
independence, 105–106
individuation process, 158
inheritance. *See* generational transfer
innovation, 119
intangible, vs. tangible, 21–22
intellectual capital, 41–42, 47, 50
intellectual giving, 138–139
intended consequences, 157
intention, 67
internal, vs. external forces, 120
intuition, 22

J

Jobs, Steve, 2
Johnson, Jamie, 83–84

K

kindness, random acts of, 140–142
knowledge, giving role, 137

L

The Last Lecture (Pausch), 66
leaders, legacy of, 133
legacy
   vs. estate planning, 20–21
   of leaders, 133
   living, vs. leaving of, 1–2
   spiritual dimensions of, 4
   wealth decisions in, 3
legacy message, 123
"The Legacy of Steve Jobs" (Herzlinger), 2–3
legal issues, vs. wisdom, 6
Les Miserables (Hugo), 130
life cycle, stages of, 90–91

life IQ
vs. financial IQ, 106–112
practices for children, 116–122
practices for parents, 112–116
principles in, 111–112
life trials, benefits of, 119–120
listening, 81–82, 160
love, giving from, 129–130, 140

M

Malloch, Theodore Roosevelt, 44
Marriott family, 150–151
material dimension, 7, 29–36, 109
materialism, 58, 60–61, 115, 118, 122
Maxwell, John C., 133
meaning, 3, 62, 65, 157–158
mental legacies, 83
mentoring, 138–139
microfinance, 137
mission statements, 33–34
modeling behavior, 112–113, 116, 131–132
money
attitudes/beliefs about, 83–85, 100, 117
communication about, 122–123
hedonic treadmill and, 60–61
as magnifying glass, 5
psychology and, 67–68, 114–115, 120
purpose of, 56
pursuit of (see materialism)
Monroy, Caine, 141–142
morphogenesis, 159
Morris, John, 136
Mullick, Nirvan, 142

N

navigational tools, 9–10, 16–18, 156
needs, vs. wants, 113, 117–118
negotiation, among family members, 161
networking, giving role, 137, 139
net worth, FISHS framework for, 40–46
next generation
    definitions, 100–103
    family business succession, 150
    life IQ principles, 116–122
    practices for parents of, 112–116
    watching of, by parents, 121
next-generation preparation. *See also* generational transfer
    case history, 103–104
    challenges of, 99–100
    communication role, 122–125
    financial, vs. life IQ, 106–112
    as multigenerational, 103–104
    overview of, 125
    practices for children, 116–122
    practices for parents, 112–116
    preparedness definition, 102–103
Nicholson, Nigel, 147
Norton, Michael. I., 63

O

obstacles, benefits of, 119–120
openness, 160
opportunities, 63, 122–123
Orlando, Richard J., 3–4, 34–36, 136
ownership shift, 104–106

P

parents/parenting, 102–104, 113, 121, 150, 158
passion, 116, 121–122, 139–140
Pausch, Randy, 66

per capita vs. *per stirpes* distribution, 92
Perdue, Frank, 67
philanthropy, 19, 127–129. *See also* giving
planning, 1–2, 99. *See also* next-generation preparation
platinum rule, 112–113, 133–134
point of view, 90, 115–116, 133–134
positive psychology, 58–59, 62–64
prayer, making time for, 81–82
prenuptial agreements, 123
preparedness, defining, 102–103. *See also* next-generation preparation
preservation, 19
productivity, 116, 121–122
professional advisors, 19, 29, 111–112, 118–119
profession/work, 65–66, 83, 107
psychology, 58–59, 114–115, 120
purpose
    communication about, 123–124
    decision-making role, 5, 22–23
    in generational transfer planning, 76–82, 121–122
    happiness role, 65
    modeling of, 116
    of money, 56–61
    spiritual capital and, 27–28, 65–68
    in wealth decisions, 3
    in *why* questions, 32–33
The Purpose Driven Life (Warren), 132
"Purposeful Travel" (Grove, Morris, and Orlando), 136

R

random acts of kindness, 140–142
receivers
    of gifts, 134
    vs. transmitters, of wealth, 100–101
"Receiving and Giving as Spiritual Exercise" (Schervish), 30
reflection, making time for, 81–82
relationships
    assessment of, 164–166

in families, 148–153, 156–159, 160–163
happiness role, 62
wealth decisions and, 1–3
religious affiliation, 25–26. *See also* faith
resilience, 91
resources, 78–80. *See also* capitals
responsibility, 91, 104–106, 121, 122–123, 162
reverse tithing, 132
Robbins, Anthony, 21
role models, parents as, 113
roles, defining, 161

S

Schervish, Paul, 30
"Secret Fears of the Super-Rich" (Wood), 58–59
self-determination, 105–106
Seligman, Martin, 58, 62
sharing, 63, 75, 93–94, 129, 131–134, 153–156. *See also* giving
sibling relationships, 159
Sinek, Simon, 32
social capital, 42–43, 44, 47, 50
social giving, 139
Solomon, King, 59–60
spiritual assets, 44–45
spiritual capital
   assessment of, 47–48, 50
   defined, 4–5, 43–44
   equation for, 27
   of families, 111
   importance of, 23–27
   as navigational tool, 9–11, 156
   purpose and, 57, 65–68
   social capital and, 44
Spiritual Enterprise (Malloch), 44
spiritual giving, 140
spirituality
   as core virtue, 24

decision-making role, 20–23
legacy planning role, 4
vs. material dimension, 7–8, 29–36, 109
vs. religious affiliation, 25–26
vs. values, 44
The Spiritual State of the Union (Gallup study), 24–25
stages, of life cycle, 90–91
stakeholders, in families, 161
staying open, 160
storytelling, 114
Stovall, John, 107–108
strengths, giving role, 139–140
success, definitions of, 116
succession statistics, 149
systems framework, for family businesses, 156–159

T

talent, giving of, 134–136, 139–140
tangible, vs. intangible, 21–22
taxes, 6, 19, 89, 129–130
team building, in families, 164
temporal nature, 8, 29–30
third generation, transfer of wealth to, 72–73
The Third Jesus (Chopra), 28
time, giving of, 134–136
transcendence, 8, 24, 29–30
transfer, of wealth, 86–88, 89–92. *See also* generational transfer
transitions, handling, 163
transmitters, vs. receivers, of wealth, 100–101
transparency, 124
trust, 21, 73, 83, 91, 163

U

The Ultimate Gift (Stovall), 107–108
underachievement, fear of, 110, 116
unexpected events, 19, 157
unintended consequences, 157

V

values
    communication about, 123–124
    decision-making role, 3, 5, 22–23, 76–82
    identifying, 77–78
    shared in families, 111
    spirituality and, 27–28, 44
    in *why* questions, 32–33
vertical dimensions, of generational transfer, 88
volunteering, 139–140

W

wants, vs. needs, 113, 117–118
Warren, Rick, 132
wealth, as financial capital, 5
wealth creators, vs. inheritors, 121–122
Weiner, Eric, 25–26
why questions, 9–10
wisdom, vs. law, 6
Wood, Graeme, 58–59
work ethic, 65–66, 83, 107